Family Violence

Family Violence

Look for these and other books in the Lucent Overview Series:

Abortion	Homeless Children
Acid Rain	Homelessness
Adoption	Illegal Immigration
Advertising	Illiteracy
Alcoholism	Immigration
Animal Rights	Juvenile Crime
Artificial Organs	Memory
The Beginning of Writing	Mental Illness
The Brain	Militias
Cancer	Money
Censorship	Multicultural America
Child Abuse	Ocean Pollution
Children's Rights	Oil Spills
Cities	The Olympic Games
The Collapse of the Soviet Union	Organ Transplants
Cults	Ozone
Dealing with Death	The Palestinian-Israeli Accord
Death Penalty	Pesticides
Democracy	Police Brutality
Drug Abuse	Population
Drugs and Sports	Poverty
Drug Trafficking	Prisons
Eating Disorders	Rain Forests
Elections	The Rebuilding of Bosnia
Endangered Species	Recycling
The End of Apartheid in South Africa	The Reunification of Germany
Energy Alternatives	Schools
Espionage	Smoking
Ethnic Violence	Space Exploration
Euthanasia	Special Effects in the Movies
Extraterrestrial Life	Sports in America
Family Violence	Suicide
Gangs	The UFO Challenge
Garbage	The United Nations
Gay Rights	The U.S. Congress
Genetic Engineering	The U.S. Presidency
The Greenhouse Effect	Vanishing Wetlands
Gun Control	Vietnam
Hate Groups	Women's Rights
Hazardous Waste	World Hunger
The Holocaust	Zoos

Family Violence

by Janice M. Yuwiler

LUCENT Overview Series

LUCENT BOOKS ®

THOMSON
™
GALE

San Diego • Detroit • New York • San Francisco • Cleveland • New Haven, Conn. • Waterville, Maine • London • Munich

© 2004 by Lucent Books. Lucent Books is an imprint of The Gale Group, Inc.,
a division of Thomson Learning, Inc.

Lucent Books® and Thomson Learning™ are trademarks used herein under license.

For more information, contact
Lucent Books
27500 Drake Rd.
Farmington Hills, MI 48331-3535
Or you can visit our Internet site at http://www.gale.com

LIBRARY OF CONGRESS CATALOGING-IN-PUBLICATION DATA

Yuwiler, Janice M.
    Family voilence/by Janice M. Yuwiler.
        p. cm — (Lucent overview series)
Summary: Examines issues related to child abuse, battered wives, and other family violence concerns, how they effect families and society, and what can be done about
them.
Includes bibliographical references and index.
    ISBN 1-59018-189-1 (hardback : alk. paper)
1. Family violence—Juvenile literature. [1. Family violence.] I. Title. II. Series.
    HV6626.Y88 2004
    362.82'92—dc22
                                                                    2003020198

Printed in the United States of America

Contents

Introduction

NOT ALL HOMES are happy places. For some people, home is a dangerous and frightening place. Ally's story is similar to that of many abuse survivors. Ally was frequently beaten by her alcoholic mother and as a result was afraid to go home. Ally remembers, "I used to get this twisted feeling in my gut when the school bus was about to drop me back at home."[1] Behind the closed doors of homes like Ally's, family members hurt each other. When abuse occurs among members of a family it is called family violence.

Child abuse, domestic violence, and elder abuse all fall under the heading of family violence. Unlike other forms of violent crime, in cases of family violence, the very people who would ordinarily be expected to love and protect the victim are the ones who cause the pain. In addition, the violent family member often hurts the victim more than once. Family violence, then, frequently is an ongoing phenomenon.

The ties between abuser and victim are often strong. The relationship is typically that of parent and child, husband and wife, or sister and brother. These family ties bind and confuse. Often the victim both loves and wants to escape the abuser. In the words of one battered woman, "I lived my life in fear, torn by my feelings for him and my terror that he would beat me again."[2]

Those who experience family violence often suffer physical and emotional problems that continue long after the abuse ends. According to the report of the American

Psychological Association's Presidential Task Force on Violence and the Family,

> Both clinical experience and psychological research demonstrate that violence and abuse within the family have real and significant effects on individuals, families, communities, and society. Many of these effects are long lasting. In fact, family violence may underlie and cause more complex psychological damage than other forms of personal violence and may be at the root of many current social problems.[3]

A pervasive problem

Both men and women abuse family members. Men beat their girlfriends, attack their wives, and abuse their children and elderly parents. Every day, at least three women are killed by their husbands or boyfriends.

Women also abuse family members, however, often by neglecting them. In the year 2000, mothers were responsible for 47 percent of the children suffering from neglect. Women also physically abuse their victims. In fact, 32 percent of the children who were physically abused in the year 2000 were abused by their mothers.

Children may also abuse members of their family. Sometimes they attack siblings, cousins, or other younger relatives. Adolescent children may even abuse their parents. One parent talks about life with her teenage daughter, saying, "My daughter was locking me in closets, putting her fists through the walls and raging on a daily basis."[4]

Experts estimate that well over 4 million people suffer from family violence in the United States each year. Over 1 million children, 1.5 million women, 835,000 men, and 1 million elders suffer from some form of abuse at the hands of family members. Even more Americans witness acts of family violence. As large as these numbers are, no one knows if they represent the full extent of family violence. This is because family violence is mostly hidden behind the closed doors of home. Those who are abused rarely talk about the abuse, even with other family members. Abusers frequently threaten their victims with additional violence if they do tell. Those who are abused may also be

Family violence, including domestic violence, is a pervasive problem throughout the world. Because many victims of such abuse maintain silence, the full extent of the problem is unknown.

embarrassed that they could not protect themselves or fear they will not be believed. Even when a victim is forced to seek medical care, he or she usually lies about how the injuries occurred, either out of fear of reprisal or to protect the abuser from legal or social consequences.

This code of silence makes the problem of family violence difficult to address. Since most people hesitate to invade a family's privacy, the violence often continues without interference. Many times the abuse is discovered only when the victim is killed or very seriously injured.

Society is struggling with how to best prevent family violence. Long-standing beliefs about family roles can cause well-intended laws and programs to fail to protect those who are abused. To address this problem, efforts are under way to educate the community and professionals about the reality of family violence and what can be done to break the cycle. Collaboration is growing across disciplines to coordinate services and family violence prevention efforts. There is still much to learn—and to do—if society is to prevent family violence from occurring. The first step is breaking the code of silence and bringing family violence into the open.

1

Family Violence and Its Impact

ABUSERS HURT MEMBERS of their family in many different ways. Some abusers punch, choke, kick, shake, or burn their victims. Others may deprive their victims of sleep, food, or clothing in order to wear down their victims' physical and emotional strength. Many abusers tell their victims they are ugly, stupid, and worthless. Some abusers even force their victims to perform sexual acts against the victims' will.

Often, the violence that occurs within the home takes more than one form. Jessica Cameronchild in *An Autobiography of Violence* talks about her experience of abuse as a child:

> Allowing a door to slam, dropping a utensil at dinner, being too slow, using the "wrong" tone of voice, failing to maintain eye contact, not standing up straight enough, and laughing too loudly were all likely to incur severe beatings. We [Jessica and her siblings] were slapped and spanked with a stick daily and every few months received injuries that required medical attention. We were constantly . . . told how stupid and unloveable we were and threatened with murder and torture. Sometimes our parents threatened to abandon us.[5]

Although the specific acts vary, the patterns are enough alike that experts have defined four main types of abuse: physical abuse, sexual abuse, neglect, and emotional abuse. Most family violence falls into at least one of these four categories.

Physical abuse

Examples of physical abuse are numerous. They include kicking, biting, shaking, burning, choking, and punching. The abuser may use his or her fists, knives, baseball bats, belts, burning cigarettes, hot water, or guns. In short, the abuser will use anything available that can hurt his or her victim.

Physical abuse can cause physical harm, and the harm caused by physical abuse can last long after the violence has ended. Survivors of physical abuse may suffer hearing loss, blindness, permanent brain damage—or worse. Genese, age fifteen, says, "I had a friend who died from her boyfriend beating her so much."[6] Those who survive abuse may have broken or missing teeth, permanent pain, and lasting physical scars.

Physical abuse can take many forms. Pictured are a child's feet exhibiting second-degree burns, the work of an abusive parent.

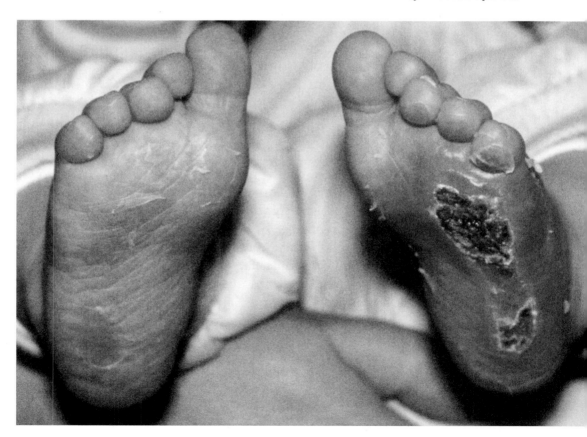

Sexual abuse

Sexual abuse includes unwanted touching of private parts or sexual acts. Sexual abuse can take place between an adult and child or between siblings, teens, or adults. Sexual abuse can even occur between spouses when one partner forces his or her desires on the other.

Sexual abuse can be confusing. Terri, age eleven, talks about her experience with sexual abuse at the hands of her foster dad. Terri did not like what he was doing, but was not sure what it meant. She explains, "When I got back from school, he'd bring me into the bathroom and start feelin' me up. . . . He'd tell me to touch him and he'd put his fingers in me, you know. I just did it. I did what he told me. For all I knew, he was tryin' to tell me he loved me."[7]

Sexual abuse can leave injuries that are harder to see but are just as long lasting. Survivors of sexual abuse can have trouble touching or being touched by others. They often have difficulty forming close relationships with others; becoming involved in an intimate dating relationship is particularly hard. Sexual abuse can be a onetime event, but it often continues for years.

Neglect

Neglect can also have long lasting effects. Neglect occurs when abusers fail to provide for the basic needs of their victims. Neglect is the most common type of child and elder abuse. Abusers may withhold food, water, clothing, or shelter from their victims. They may refuse to give their victims attention or affection. Abusers may delay needed medical treatment or even permanently abandon their victims. In the first case of child neglect to be brought to court in the United States, in 1874, Mary Ellen, age eight, testified how her adoptive mother ignored her need for social contact, affection, and clothing:

> I am never allowed to play with any children or to have any company whatever. . . . I have no recollection of ever having been kissed by any one—have never been kissed by mamma. I have never been taken on my mamma's lap and caressed or petted. I never dared to speak to anybody, because if I did I

Victims of neglect often do not receive their most basic needs, like food, water, clothing, or shelter. Neglect can also cause deep and lasting psychological trauma.

would get whipped. I have never had, to my recollection, any more clothing than I have at present—a calico dress and shirt. I have seen stockings and other clothes in our room, but was not allowed to put them on. Whenever mamma went out I was locked up in the bedroom.[8]

Neglect can be deadly. Victims of neglect can die from malnutrition, exposure to the elements, or lack of needed medical treatment. Even when victims of neglect survive, they still may suffer brain damage or stunted growth caused by lack of food.

Emotional abuse

Unlike neglect, in which the victim's emotional needs may be ignored, emotional abuse consists of deliberate attempts to erode the victim's emotional or mental well-being. Verbal abuse is a common tool. An abuser may tell his wife or girlfriend she is stupid, ugly, worthless, or crazy to destroy her self-confidence. Kati, age fifteen, remembers the experiences of some of her friends: "I've had friends that have had problems, more mental than physical. Like the guy will try to brainwash her, make her think she's not going to be anything without him, or if he's not in her life, she won't have anybody. He won't let her think of any other person, she can't talk to or barely look at other guys or he'll get mad."[9]

Like many abusers, perpetrators of emotional abuse will try to isolate their victim from friends and family so that the victim becomes dependent on the abuser. The abuser may tell the victim her family does not love her to break her family ties. He may tell her friends that she does not want to see them anymore. Sometimes the line between emotional and physical abuse blurs. For example, abusers may stalk their victims to control and terrorize them or they may torment them by refusing to let them sleep, sit down, or go to the bathroom. One child's aunt used to make her stand on the stairs with her hands behind her back from seven or eight in the morning until after eleven o'clock at night.

Emotional abuse can have long-term psychological and physical effects. Many survivors suffer from low self-esteem, have trouble trusting other people, and experience depression. They may experience physical symptoms such as constant headaches, stomach problems, or even ulcers. Some survivors, seeking to dull their emotional and physical pain, become addicted to alcohol or drugs.

Secrecy

No matter what the type of abuse, victims rarely talk about what is happening to them. Sometimes the abuse is kept secret because the abuser has threatened terrible consequences if the victim tells anyone. Anita, a survivor of sexual abuse, remembers what her father said: "He told me that if people found out they would probably send him to jail; that maybe my mother would kill him or kill all of us, or maybe she would kill herself. I had a very strong message that's still with me: if I tell, somebody dies."[10]

Sometimes those who are abused have trouble believing that the abuse is happening. Lorraine, who was beaten and sexually abused by her husband, says, "I didn't know how to tell anyone what was happening to me. I don't know if anyone would have believed me because I could hardly believe it myself. . . . I considered the experiences I was having a nightmare."[11]

Others feel that they should have been able to protect themselves or want to protect their abusers. In these cases, survivors may not report the abuse because they are worried what people would think about them or their abuser. Casey says about life with her husband, "If I said anything about the way he really was, it would have made him look bad and it would have made me look ridiculous. So I just kept quiet."[12]

Sometimes, too, victims keep silent because they believe the abuse is their fault or that they deserve the abuse. They do not want others to know how horrible they must be to be experiencing the type of abuse they suffer. Lorraine remembers thinking that she had somehow brought the battering on herself: "I suffered so much, but I was ashamed to tell anybody about it. I had never heard of this happening to anyone I knew and I thought I had done something terrible to deserve such treatment."[13]

The abuser in control

The victim, however, is not the cause of the abuse. The abuse does not occur because of something the victim did or did not do, regardless of what the abuser says. It is the abuser who is in control of the situation. In the words of one abuser, "She couldn't make me hit her if I didn't want to."[14]

The abuser, therefore, decides when, where, and how to be abusive, often claiming that the victim did something

Abusers are manipulative and often try to make the victim feel that he or she deserves to be punished.

wrong and needs to be punished. Brenda recalls the many things her husband used as excuses for attacking her:

> Anything would set him off. Maybe I wasn't somewhere he wanted me to be, or he saw me talking, or I got a letter that was addressed specifically to me, or I took too long at the store. . . . He never had a good explanation. He'd say it was stress or his mother was pushing him too much, but mostly it was me. If I wouldn't have said something in that tone of voice, or if I would have done something I was specifically supposed to do, it wouldn't have happened.[15]

In fact, far from bringing violence upon themselves, victims do everything in their power to please their abuser and prevent the violence. They change their behavior to do and be exactly what they think the abuser wants, but they rarely succeed. Paula remembers, "He beat me because dinner wasn't ready when he came home, so I made sure it was on the table the minute he came through the door. He threw the food on the floor and beat me anyway."[16]

Another abuse survivor, Gertrude, kept trying to figure out how to prevent the violence: "If I hadn't gotten hit the day before, I tried to do and say everything the next day in exactly the same way I had done or said it the day before. I thought 'that must be the answer.' It never did any good. Eventually, I saw that no matter what I said or did, I was going to be hit."[17]

Co-occurrence

Often, abusers victimize more than one member of a family. This is known as co-occurrence. Approximately half the men who frequently beat their wives also beat their children. The more violent the man, the more likely he is to abuse both his wife and children. The same is true for women. A national survey found that more than a third of the mothers who continually abuse their husbands also abuse their male children.

About half of the men who batter their spouses also abuse their children. Abused family members live in terror, uncertain when the next violent outburst will occur.

In addition, women who are abused are more likely to abuse their children. Thomas remembers his experience: "My stepfather had been beating my mother on a regular basis, about two to three times a month. Usually, when she got beaten by him, she ended up beating [me] before the week was out."[18] In fact, co-occurrence is so common that the U.S. Advisory Board on Child Abuse suggests that domestic violence—that is, one spouse or partner abusing the other—may be the most important factor in predicting deaths from child abuse and neglect.

Costs of family violence

Family violence not only causes injury and death but impacts society in general. Adult abuse victims miss work, resulting in lost productivity. Police and other government agencies are overwhelmed trying to protect abuse survivors, and courts are busy with the placement of abused children, the prosecution of abusers, protection orders for battered spouses, and criminal proceedings against caregivers who have abused older adults. Mental health clinics, schools, prisons, and police are all called on to work with abusers and victims of family violence. The actual cost in dollars is enormous. The state of Colorado alone estimated that it spends $402 million each year just to provide services to abused children and deal with the long-term consequences of child abuse, including disabilities, substance abuse, and criminal justice. Nationally, the cost of health care just for survivors of domestic violence is $5.8 billion.

Long lasting

No matter what form it takes, family violence has impacts that are felt long after the abuse ends. For example, the physical injuries Nell's husband inflicted left her unable to work and support herself. Nell is not alone. Many abuse survivors suffer permanent physical disabilities. Family violence can cause arthritis, chronic neck or back pain, brain damage, vision and hearing problems, disfigurement, and sexually transmitted diseases. Nora J. Baladerian testified before the U.S. Advisory Board on Child Abuse and Neglect that up to 28 percent of all disabled persons in the United States may have been disabled because of child abuse and neglect.

Family violence can also cause lasting psychological damage. Casey, a survivor of abuse, describes the impact of being locked in a closet by her husband: "Being locked in the closet [several times] left me with serious claustrophobia. I'm terrified of any enclosed space, of riding in elevators or small cars. I can't stand to be in an airplane. This is a problem which has had considerable effect on my career because of the amount of traveling I am obliged to do."[19]

In fact, psychological damage from family violence is common. Almost half of domestic violence survivors suffer symptoms of anxiety or a disorder known as posttraumatic stress disorder. They may experience nightmares, upset stomachs, heart palpitations, insomnia, dizziness, trembling, and muscle aches. In addition, 29 percent of women who attempt suicide are victims of domestic violence. It can take years to recover from the psychological effects of abuse, and some scars may never disappear. As Casey says, "My mind was unbelievably messed up. . . . I finally [after years] recovered sufficiently to feel comfortable talking with people."[20]

Family violence can also leave survivors in poverty. Laurel's experience is not unusual. Laurel's husband stole her life savings, destroyed her credit, and left her without any money to live on. Older adults can lose their homes and life savings when abusers trick them into signing documents or giving the abuser access to their bank accounts.

In addition, family violence can have a traumatic effect on those who witness it. It is estimated that 3.3 to 10 million children witness domestic violence each year. Young children in homes where domestic violence occurs can be overwhelmed when the two people they depend on fight. Angie remembers, "[My father] was abusive towards my mother. I'd see him slap her around, push her, knock her down. . . . It was frightening to watch. I would beg him not to hurt her, and I would cry. Then I'd get spanked for crying. After a while, I learned not to cry."[21]

Victims of domestic violence like this woman commonly suffer from anxiety or posttraumatic stress disorder, even years after the abuse has ended.

Older children who witness family violence may decide that they are big enough to step in and protect the victim from the abuser. In their effort to stop the abuse, however, they can become a target themselves. The dilemma these children face is wrenching. They can be seriously hurt or killed if they try to intervene, but doing nothing can tear them apart emotionally.

The unpredictability of abuse

Adding to the emotional tumult for members of abusive families is the unpredictability of the abuse. Members of families in which violence occurs live in constant fear of an attack. Jessica Cameronchild in *An Autobiography of Violence* describes what life is like for a battered child:

> Being a battered child means never knowing the consequences of a gesture, facial expression, or request. Sometimes a gift of flowers is received affectionately and sometimes it's

dashed down with a tirade of abuse. Sometimes a request for gum is a "good idea" and sometimes it's "proof of your horrid greediness and irresponsible lack of concern for the cost of dental care." Sometimes looking sad is met with friendly concern, and sometimes you're berated and punished for being ungrateful. But you just never know.[22]

Such uncertainty forces abuse survivors to be hypersensitive to the abuser's emotions. At the same time, survivors must overlook their own feelings and needs. For survival, they learn to dull their senses. This means that abused children may not learn the social skills they need to be successful in society.

Breaking the cycle

One of the tragic effects of family violence is the way it can be passed on from generation to generation. Children who are abused, or who witness abuse, often grow up to have abusive relationships as adults. They have learned from experience that those who supposedly love them the most are the people who hit, yell, or degrade them. One psychiatrist, Dr. William Rader, says, "As adults, abused children tend to look for the same message they were sent in their childhoods. A woman will marry a man who will beat her because she feels this is what she deserves."[23]

Vicki's experience built on what she learned about relationships growing up in an abusive home:

When I got a little bit older, I wanted to fall in love; but I didn't feel I could trust anyone. I got myself into some terrible situations. I was always going out with the most dangerous men I could find . . . men who made my [abusive] father look like a wimp. Even at that time I could tell I wasn't making healthy choices. . . . I hadn't learned the proper social dynamics. I'd never seen two people live as partners. I'd never witnessed a healthy love.[24]

Other children who were abused or who witnessed abuse grow up to abuse others. They treat their children the way they were treated. They treat their spouses the way they saw their parents treat each other. Studies have found that boys who grow up witnessing domestic violence are more likely to abuse their partners. This is especially true if by

Children, especially young boys, who grow up witnessing family violence are more likely to become abusive as adults.

witnessing their father's or stepfather's actions they are taught that women are inferior, that women's feelings are unimportant, or that men should have the last word in an argument. B.J. remembers, "I got to the point where I was just as abusive toward my mother as [my father] was. That's what I was taught to do."[25]

Abused children often do not have another model to follow. As a result, the American Psychological Association notes, "The best predictor of future violence is previous violence. Children who experience multiple acts of violence or more than one kind of violence are at a greater risk for continuing the 'cycle of violence.'"[26]

Experts contend that the cycle can be broken. Not all children grow up to abuse others or be abused by their partners. There are many factors involved, but an important step is to break the code of silence and get help to families suffering from abuse. To this end, experts are working to increase public knowledge about abuse and build systems to identify and assist families suffering from family violence.

Publisher
Health Communcation
1995
Deerfield Beach FL

2

Child Abuse

W$_{\text{ITH}}$ EXPERTS ESTIMATING that more than 1 million children experience some form of violence at home each year, child abuse is clearly a very real problem in the United States. Dealing with child abuse, however, offers a number of challenges. Reluctance among people to interfere with how parents raise their children, confusion about how best to intervene, and a lack of resources all hamper efforts to address child abuse.

A choice left to parents

The choice of how to discipline a child is left to the parents. Relatives, neighbors, teachers, and the police are all hesitant to interfere with parental discipline. This reluctance to interfere allows abuse to continue, sometimes to the point where it results in death. An example is that of a little girl in New York who was beaten by her mother's boyfriend. According to Dr. Michael Baden, director of forensic services of the New York State Police, "She was beaten intermittently for more than a week. Many neighbors saw her badly marked face. But the neighbors did not think it was their business, and the family was not reported. Only when the child was killed did the beatings come to the attention of authorities."[27]

Who is at risk?

Young children are at the greatest risk of being killed by their parents. Eighty-five percent of the children who die from child abuse are under five years old. Almost half are infants. Even among older children, however, child abuse can be deadly. In cases of children under twelve years old who were murdered, more than half of the victims were killed by their parents.

Child abuse occurs at all levels of society and in all types of families: rich, poor, and middle class. Child abuse also occurs in all racial, ethnic, and religious groups. Only in cases of serious neglect or severe physical abuse does poverty seem to play a role. In these cases, the stress and frustration associated with poverty seem to operate in combination with other factors, such as caring for more than

The youngest, most helpless victims of child abuse are more likely to die as a result of the abuse than older children.

four children, being a young parent, abusing drugs, and being isolated with few sources of emotional support. In fact, 50 to 80 percent of the families being investigated or treated for child abuse have at least one parent who is using alcohol or drugs. Alcohol and drug use can make family violence worse. Some abusers are so worried about getting alcohol or drugs that they neglect themselves and their families. Suzanne remembers about her father, "After a few hours of his nightly drinking, he'd get an attack of 'the means.' We wouldn't know what to expect, exactly, but it was never good."[28]

There are also personal factors that seem to increase the risk for child abuse. Parents who were abused as children themselves or who witnessed abuse may have learned to use violence as a way to control others. These parents are more likely to abuse their children. In a real sense, the tendency to abuse can be a legacy that continues for generations.

Abusive parents also tend to have low self-esteem. Many have few friends, coworkers, relatives, or professionals they can turn to for support. As a result, many abusive parents look to their children for love and support. In the words of one abusive mother, "I have never felt really loved all my life. When the baby was born, I thought he would love me; but when he cried all the time, it meant he didn't love me, so I hit him."[29]

Abusive parents often expect too much of their children. According to pediatrician Ray E. Helfer at Michigan State University,

> These [abused] children find themselves in a world of unrealistic expectations. Their parents have little understanding of childhood and make demands that are far in excess of a child's capabilities. Babies shouldn't cry much . . . two year olds should shape up, not explore the cupboards and pull out the pots, not spill anything and eat well. "Look after *me*," the child is told by the parent. . . . From success at school, to caring for mom and dad, the demands are *extreme*.[30]

Thomas remembers when he was a boy of about seven years old, "I'd go home and clean up the whole kitchen. I'd

Drug use is common in families in which violence occurs. Consumed with their habits, drug abusers frequently neglect or lash out at their families.

get the dirty diapers and wash them by hand. I'd sweep the yard. I only wanted to do good. I just wanted to please my mother, but I never could."[31]

As much as abused children try to please, they will fail to meet their parents' impossible expectations. And failure brings on punishment. These children are told they are no good and never will be. They set aside their own needs to take care of their parents but are left feeling unloved and unworthy, and rarely have their own needs met. Many abused children grow into needy adults with low self-esteem, and the cycle of unrealistic expectations and child abuse continues.

Impact of child abuse

Children react differently to abuse. Some abused children are aggressive. Others are withdrawn and anxious. No matter how they react, most abused children have difficulty trusting others. They may also have trouble feeling empathy. That is, they find it difficult to understand the perspectives and feelings of others. As a result, they can find it hard to make friends.

As they grow older, abused children tend not to do well in school. They may have difficulty sleeping. They may find themselves feeling depressed and even thinking about suicide. If they have been sexually abused, they may have trouble forming long-term relationships. Abused children may develop eating disorders or abuse alcohol or drugs. They are also more likely to commit crimes, have emotional problems, or run away from home. Gary, for exam-

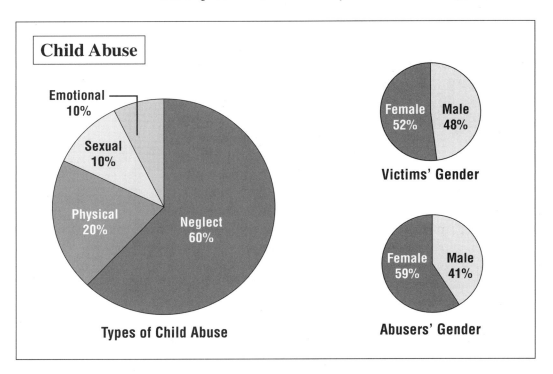

Child Abuse

Emotional 10%
Sexual 10%
Physical 20%
Neglect 60%

Types of Child Abuse

Female 52% Male 48%

Victims' Gender

Female 59% Male 41%

Abusers' Gender

ple, was full of anger over the severe beatings he had endured from his father. For years, Gary used pills and alcohol to dull the pain from his memories. Gary was lucky. Unlike his abused brothers, who eventually committed suicide, Gary was able to come to grips with his anger and stop using drugs and alcohol.

In the end, the impact of abuse depends on many factors. The age of the child is important because children learn different skills at different ages. The home and school environment, as well as the type and frequency of abuse, will also affect the long-term impact.

Some children, interestingly, appear to experience relatively few problems as a result of abuse. These children are called resilient. Professionals are very interested in learning what protects these children. So far, research shows that one of the most powerful protective factors is having an adult who listens to the abused child and helps him or her feel protected. This adult can be a teacher, relative, or neighbor. It does not matter who the adult is. What is important is that the adult believes the child and offers him or her support. Dee recalls her childhood, "I would never have gotten through those years if it hadn't been for a wonderful couple, Bill and Donna. . . . They would come over and take me out of the house when it got too bad and I couldn't take it any more. Without ever putting my father down, they really helped me through. And they were always there to listen."[32]

Battered child syndrome

As the research on resiliency suggests, intervention offers hope for abused children. Indeed, getting help to abused children has become a priority for many child advocates and professionals. Pediatricians now make a practice of keeping an eye out for a pattern of injuries in their patients that is called battered child syndrome: Children who have been physically abused who exhibit a pattern of old, healing, and new injuries that are visible at the same time. Typically, on each visit the doctor hears a different story about how the child received the injuries. This vigilance is relatively new. As a child, Jessica remembers going to the same school and doctor each month with injuries and never being asked why she and her siblings were hurt so often:

> Throughout these years we were attending the same school, with many of the same teachers. We also visited the same pediatrician month after month. He was a friend of our father's and was usually given plausible explanations for our injuries. . . . We were all straight "A" students and extremely well-behaved. No one seemed to recognize that there was something unhealthy about our model behavior. No one questioned how such capable children could hurt themselves so often.[33]

Pediatricians are trained to be vigilant for signs of battered child syndrome. They are required by law to report any evidence of abuse.

Because abusive parents often construct plausible explanations, doctors are being trained to look beyond what they are told caused the injury to check for other healing injuries and to be sure that the injuries they see match the story given. For example, falling off a bike will not cause burn marks or new and healing welts on a child's back.

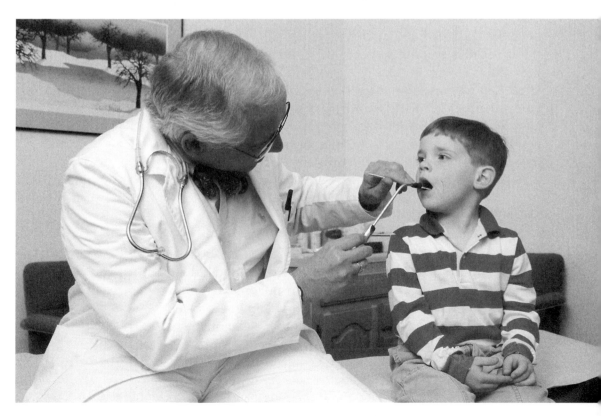

When doctors see evidence of abuse or suspect that a child is being abused, laws require them to report the case to Child Protective Services (CPS).

Child Protective Services

Child Protective Services is a local government agency responsible for investigating and responding to reported cases of child abuse. In addition to doctors, a child's teachers, psychologists, social workers, police, and school counselors are required to report suspected cases of child abuse. Child Protective Services will also take reports from anyone else who suspects a child is being abused.

A CPS investigation typically consists of a caseworker visiting the family and talking with teachers, counselors, doctors, neighbors, police, or anyone else who might know what is happening in the home. The CPS worker needs to determine the type and severity of the abuse, who the abuser is, and whether other children in the home are being abused. Based on the investigation, the caseworker decides what to do next.

Remove the child or help the family?

Deciding how to intervene to help an abused child is difficult. For example, overestimating the danger and removing the child from the home can needlessly tear apart a family. On the other hand, a child's life may be endangered if he or she is left in the home. Currently the trend is to leave the child with his or her family if the home can be made safe. This is called family preservation. Dr. Vincent de Francis, a leader in the American Humane Association, summed up this position in 1955 when he said, "The best way to rescue a child is to rescue the family for the child."[34]

The federal government came out in support of family preservation with the passage of the Adoption Assistance and Child Welfare Act of 1980. This law requires states to make reasonable efforts to keep families together and avoid placing children in substitute care. In practice this means that typically a caseworker is assigned to work with the family to provide home-based counseling, parent education, anger management, techniques for coping with behavior problems, communication skills, and links to community resources and services, including help with transportation, housing, clothing, and emergency funds. Some programs last for four to six weeks. They provide intensive support for up to twenty hours a week and include access to the caseworker twenty-four hours a day. Other programs are less intensive but provide help for a longer period of time.

Studies of family preservation programs show mixed results. Cases come to light from time to time of children who were left in homes that in hindsight were clearly too dangerous. In other cases, children have been removed from homes then returned to their parents only to be killed. As one expert commented, attempts to preserve families at all costs ignore "the uncomfortable truth that some parents are beyond the reach of even the best treatment programs."[35]

Foster care

When a parent cannot provide for the child's safety or presents an obvious threat, the child is removed from the home. In many states, the majority of these children are placed in foster care. Foster parents are licensed by the county or state. Their homes have been checked for basic health and safety standards, and the parents have received some training on how to take care of children. Foster parents agree to raise and care for the child temporarily until a better or permanent placement can be found. Usually these children are eventually returned to their parents, are adopted into a new family, or leave the foster care system at age eighteen when they are legally considered adults.

Though many children placed in foster care find themselves in loving, supportive homes, the system does not always work. Most foster families try to help their foster children, but some foster parents abuse the children entrusted to their care. Terri was placed in a foster home when she was six years old. When she tried to tell the school nurse and her social worker that her foster father was sexually abusing her, they would not listen. In Terri's words, "[My social worker] just didn't care; as long as I was somewhere, it didn't matter what was happening to me. If I was being raped, or gettin' beat on, it wasn't no big deal, as long as I had a roof over my head."[36]

Sometimes, too, the very nature of foster care means that children are moved from one foster family to another, never staying in any one place for long. This can happen when an unsuccessful attempt is made to reunite the child with his or her parents. Other times the foster parents cannot continue caring for the child. James talks about his experience growing up in foster care: "I was mostly a foster kid, because a long time ago, when I was about three, they took me away from my mom—I don't know why—maybe she just couldn't take care of me. So I

A girl skates into the loving arms of her adoptive father. Many abused children are not fortunate enough to be adopted, and spend years in the foster care system.

lived in foster homes. I lived in thirteen different foster homes, all in Illinois."[37]

The growing number of child abuse cases in the United States and the shortage of funding makes it difficult for Child Protective Services to deal with the problem.

Kinship care

The pressure to find temporary homes for abused children and the shortage of foster parents has prompted some CPS agencies to place children with relatives instead of foster care. These placements are called kinship care. Charlene Ingram, a social work administrator in the

Philadelphia Department of Human Services, notes that kinship care "provides continuity, lessens the trauma of separation, preserves family ties, and offers growth and development within the context of a child's culture and community."[38]

Placing children in kinship care is in keeping with the trend for family preservation and recognizes the strengths of individual families. Although some experts fear that relatives may not be safe caregivers because of the intergenerational cycle of abuse, one of the rare studies of children in foster and kinship care found that children in kinship care feel as safe as children in foster care do. However, children in kinship care were more likely to say they were happier in a variety of ways than were the children in foster care.

The use of kinship care varies from state to state, with some states placing almost half their children in kinship care and others more often using traditional foster care. States also vary in the requirements kinship families must meet. In some states, the requirements for licensing and training are the same for both traditional foster care and kinship care. Other states have more flexible standards for kinship care.

An enormous burden

The many and diverse responsibilities of Child Protective Services, along with the growing number of child abuse cases each year and a shortage of funding, places an enormous burden on caseworkers. Each CPS worker has so many child abuse reports to investigate that it is hard to be thorough. According to a report of the U.S. Advisory Board on Child Abuse and Neglect, "In many jurisdictions caseloads are so high that the best CPS can do is take the complaint call, make a single visit to the home, and decide whether the complaint is founded or unfounded. Often there is no subsequent monitoring of the family."[39]

In addition, CPS workers often lack the training they need to make the difficult decisions they face every day. An extreme example is the case of a five-year-old boy in Illinois who died of malnutrition. Three different caseworkers had visited the home but had concluded he was merely small for his age. CPS agencies have tried to address the problem by creating standard procedures for caseworkers to follow that will help the majority of children. Sometimes, though, these standard procedures deny CPS workers the flexibility to respond to individual needs.

In 1997 a task force of social policy experts called the Harvard Executive Session met to suggest ways of overhauling the child protection and welfare system nationwide. Their concerns were the number of families referred to CPS (including the families who should not have been reported and the families who were missed), the fact that in many cases typical CPS interventions do not work, and the lack of services available to help families in need. The Harvard Executive Session recommended that CPS agencies share responsibilities with other partners in the community to provide different levels of response to families. Specifically, CPS should partner with criminal justice organizations to respond to high-risk cases that need governmental intervention. The responsibility to help children and families at lower risk should be addressed by community programs. For this to work there needs to be sufficient funding for these programs. In addition, such groups will need to work together to plan, fund, and deliver services that support families and address child abuse.

3

Domestic Violence

DOMESTIC VIOLENCE, WHICH is defined as abuse between members of a married or dating couple, is a serious problem in the United States today. The U.S. surgeon general reports that attacks by male partners are the leading cause of injury to women ages fifteen to forty-four. Domestic violence is also widespread. Lenore Walker, a noted authority on domestic violence, estimates that half of all women are abused by their mate at some point in their life. In addition, research shows that one-third of all female murder victims are murdered by their partners. As serious as the problem is, addressing domestic violence is challenging. Societal beliefs about the rights and roles of men and women, the complex nature of a couple's relationship, and the rewards the abuser gains by abusing his or her partner lie at the heart of this challenge.

Who is at risk?

Anyone can suffer from domestic violence. Victims are married, unmarried, divorced, or widowed. They can be in male-female or same-sex relationships; rich, poor, educated, or uneducated; and from any religious or ethnic background. Even teens can experience domestic violence. A survey of young people found that 40 percent of girls ages fourteen to seventeen know someone their age who has been hit or beaten by a boyfriend. Abusers can be doctors, lawyers, construction workers, police officers, accountants, or short-order cooks. Domestic violence is truly found at all levels of society.

Most violent abusers are male, and they come from a broad range of socioeconomic, religious, and ethnic backgrounds.

Although both men and women abuse their partners, statistics show that women partners are injured thirteen times more frequently than male partners. Among homosexuals, more abuse is found in male couples than in female couples. According to the American Psychological Association's Presidential Task Force on Violence and the Family, "Women initiate violence less frequently than men; when they do, their acts usually are in self-defense. In addition, women's violent behavior toward their intimate partners is typically less severe and less frequent, results in fewer injuries, and includes less fear-inducing intimidating and bullying behavior."[40] As a result, more women are terrified of their partners than men are.

A desire for control

Domestic violence hinges on the desire of one partner to control the other. Domestic violence expert Lundy Bancroft, who has worked with over two thousand abusive men, notes,

> The underlying goal of these abusers, whether conscious or not, is to control their female partners. They consider themselves entitled to demand service and to impose punishments when they feel that their needs are not being met. They look down on their partners as inferior to them, a view that often extends to their outlook on women in general.[41]

The Presidential Task Force on Violence and the Family reinforces this link between control and domestic violence:

> Historically, men were expected to be dominant, active, and in control. Women were expected to be submissive, passive, and dependent. . . . Men, for example, receive the false message that they have a right and a mandate to control the women and children in their families. That belief contributes significantly to men's continued use of violence to maintain power and control. Individuals, families, and society are damaged when such behavior is tolerated as being normal.[42]

Although a desire for control lies at the heart of domestic violence, alcohol or drug use can contribute to the problem. Anabolic steroids or crack cocaine can cause violent behavior, and an estimated 45 percent of male abusers were drinking prior to abusing their partner. According to Lundy Bancroft,

> Alcohol provides an abuser with an *excuse* to freely act on his desires. After a few drinks, he turns himself loose to be as insulting or intimidating as he feels inclined to be, knowing that the next day he can say, "Hey, sorry about last night, I was really trashed" or even claim to have completely forgotten the incident, and his partner, his family, or even a judge will let him off the hook.[43]

The dynamics of domestic violence

The dynamics of domestic violence are hauntingly similar across couples. Typically, the abuser is charming and loving at first. He works to bind his partner to him. Casey's story is typical: "I felt as though I had truly found my soul mate. . . . Gunter knew exactly the right things to say and do, exactly how I would react. It was nearly perfect. . . . The only difficulty I could find in our relationship was that Gunter loved me so much he simply could not bear for us to be apart."[44]

Subtly, however, the abuser works to isolate the victim. The abuser separates the victim from family, friends, and any support network. Casey recalls her husband moving the family whenever she started to set up her business and a network of friends. "Once I established myself on the West Coast, he found a reason to move to the South," she says. "Then we moved back to the Coast. It seemed as though I was always moving, always being uprooted and separated from any friends I might make."[45]

The abuser also works to make his victim dependent on him so that she will stay and continue to serve him. For example, Gunter insisted that Casey invest her money in his business. In addition, anything Casey bought was put into Gunter's name, so the house and all their possessions legally belonged to him. Casey was left dependent on Gunter for access to her own home and belongings.

The cycle of violence

For the most part, domestic violence follows what psychotherapist Lenore Walker describes as the cycle of violence. The cycle of violence has three main phases. In the tension-building phase, abusers become more critical of the victim. The couple has more arguments and the abuser's mood can change quickly. The victim tries hard to please the abuser and to stay out of his (or her) way. Encouraged by the victim's passive acceptance, however, the abuser makes less effort to control himself until he finally explodes.

The acute battering phase discharges the tension that has built up in the first phase. The accompanying explosion

can involve verbal, physical, and/or sexual abuse. It may last for minutes or days. Usually the attacks will increase in severity over time. According to Leslie A. Cantrell, author of the book *Into the Light*, "While the abuser may start out to 'teach [the victim] a lesson' . . . he usually finds that he has severely injured her."[46]

When the acute phase is over, it is followed by a period of initial shock, denial, and disbelief. Both partners find ways to rationalize the attack and minimize its seriousness. Many victims report reactions similar to those of disaster victims, with the full impact not setting in until twenty-four or forty-eight hours after the attack.

The final phase in the cycle of violence is called the honeymoon phase and is characterized by the kind and loving attention the abuser gives the victim. According to Cantrell,

A police officer responds to a domestic violence call. Many battered women are reluctant to report abuse because they fear retaliation by the abuser.

The batterer frequently begins an intense campaign to win forgiveness and to assure that the relationship will remain intact. It is common for an abuser [in the honeymoon phase] to shower his victims with elaborate gifts, flowers, and candy, to "romance" her into forgiving him, to enlist the aid of family, friends, clergy, even counselors in persuading her to maintain the status quo. Often everyone involved believes the rationalization—that he is sorry and will change, that his workload or his drinking are to blame, that his children need him, that he needs his victim's help to change. And somehow the victim begins to assume responsibility for any punishment that the batterer may receive. She sees herself as the one who must stay by her partner while he gets the help he needs so desperately.[47]

The cycle then repeats itself. With time, the honeymoon phase grows shorter and shorter and the acute battering phase grows more violent. Breaking the cycle of violence is very difficult. The victim is under the abuser's control, and he manipulates her to ensure she stays that way.

Breaking the cycle

Many advocates for battered women contend that the only hope for a battered partner is to leave the abusive relationship. They see the abused partner as trapped by a controlling abuser who minimizes and disregards her needs and feelings. An abuser who puts his needs first and is willing to use force and manipulation to achieve his desires is unlikely to change his behavior.

Not all abused women agree with this view, however. Some battered women do not want to be pressured into leaving their husbands and blamed for making bad choices. Ruth Schulder, a social worker in New York City, says, "Nobody has the right to say to a woman, 'You can't be with this guy.' So we have to deal with the reality."[48] The reality is that some survivors make calculated decisions to stay with their abuser. Sometimes an abused woman is scared that her abuser will kill her if she leaves. Sometimes she is afraid she cannot make it on her own, or if she is an immigrant that she might be deported. Sometimes she stays for the same reasons other couples stay in less than perfect relationships. She stays for the children, because of her marriage vows, or because she loves her partner.

Moreover, leaving a domestic violence situation can be extremely dangerous. Indeed, the survivor and her children are in more danger when they attempt to leave than at any other time in the relationship. Faced with the prospect of losing control over his partner, some abusers will stalk, threaten, and even kill their victims when they leave. Brenda, a survivor of domestic violence, remembers, "I left and went into hiding, but even that didn't work. . . . He tracked me down and showed up at the parking lot of the country club where I worked. He caused a scene, smashing the

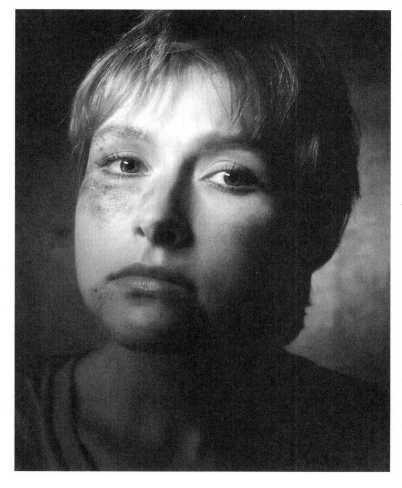

There are many different reasons why battered women stay in abusive relationships. Some victims fear that their lives are in jeopardy if they leave.

windshield of my car. Robert said that if I didn't come home to him, the next time it wouldn't be my windshield getting smashed; it would be my head."[49]

Domestic violence shelters

Many survivors who decide to leave despite the danger flee to domestic violence shelters. The types of services offered by these shelters vary. Most not only supply food, clothing, and a place to stay but also provide counseling, safety planning, and referrals for legal and health services. They frequently run emergency hotlines and conduct crisis counseling and support groups. Those who operate shelters also try to educate their community and help people understand the dynamics of domestic violence. More and more they are reaching out to police officers, courts, and doctors to teach professionals how to protect and assist survivors of domestic violence.

Assumptions about families

Such education is needed. Police officers, judges, clergy, psychologists, and even family and friends frequently respond to abuse victims based on mistaken assumptions. They often do not understand the power and control issues of domestic violence and advise battered women to return to their husbands. Lorraine remembers the response of the police when she called them after her husband first started to beat her: "I had asked them to help me, and I tried to report the abuse, but the policeman I spoke with only told me to 'behave myself' and 'not to do things to make my husband angry.'"[50]

Like Lorraine, many battered women have been told to stop complaining about their husbands, go home, make up, and be better wives. For example, one judge in Massachusetts denied a battered woman's plea to have her husband barred from her home, saying, "I don't believe in breaking up families."[51]

Sometimes when people recognize there is a problem, they recommend that the couple attend joint counseling or use mediation. Such recommendations can be dangerous.

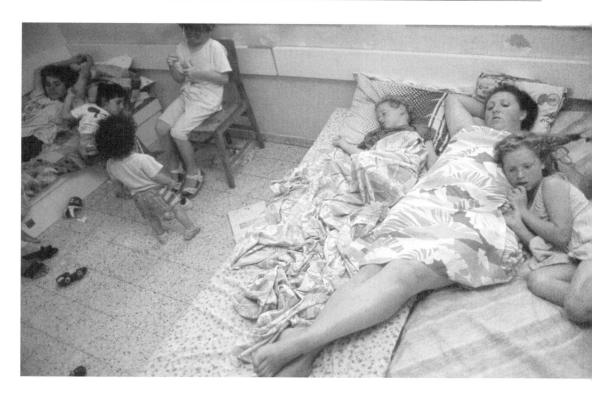

According to Lundy Bancroft, "Couples counseling sends both the abuser and the abused woman the wrong message. The abuser learns that his partner is 'pushing his buttons' and 'touching him off' and that she needs to adjust her behavior to avoid getting him so upset. This is precisely what he has been claiming all along."[52]

In addition, if the abused partner mentions something that the abuser finds embarrassing or that he feels makes him look bad, he may retaliate later. Irene, a survivor of domestic violence, remembers discussing her husband's abuse at the prompting of her therapist. Although her husband appeared remorseful in the therapist's office, he beat her in the car on the way home while screaming that he had told her never to talk about the abuse.

Domestic violence shelters provide a haven for families fleeing abuse. The shelters provide basic necessities, as well as counseling and other assistance.

Protection and restraining orders

Battered partners can seek protection from their abuser in the form of protection or restraining orders from a judge.

Such orders can require the abuser to stay away from the battered partner, her home, and her place of work. An abuser who violates the terms of the restraining order is subject to arrest and prosecution.

Protection and restraining orders, however, are only effective if police enforce them. In many cases abusers attack their partners even when protection or restraining orders are in place. For example, even though Sally had a restraining order, her former husband repeatedly broke in to her apartment, stole her money, destroyed her possessions, and beat her. The last time she called the police, it took them two hours to respond. By the time the police arrived, Sally's apartment was destroyed and she was in the hospital.

According to Jan Berliner Statman, author of *The Battered Woman's Survival Guide*, experience has made police wary of intervening in domestic violence situations:

> Most police officers will agree that domestic violence calls are among the most unpleasant and dangerous calls they have to make. Many of them have had the unfortunate experience

A restraining order is a court-issued document that requires abusers to keep away from their victims. Should an abuser violate the order, he or she is subject to arrest.

of attempting to assist a battered woman only to have her turn violently against them to protect her batterer! Or they have attempted to protect a battered woman only to have her insist that she did not need their help. Many officers do not understand the victim's fear, or the reprisals that will follow when they leave.[53]

Mandated reporting and prosecution

Survivors of domestic violence often fear retaliation if they report their abuse or press charges if their abuser is arrested. In response, many states have passed laws requiring or mandating doctors, nurses, and other professionals to report cases of domestic violence. States have also passed laws allowing for the prosecution of abusers even if the victim refuses to testify or press charges. The idea is to hold abusers accountable for their actions while protecting abuse victims from retaliation. Mandatory reporting of domestic violence also means that a report is created that can be used as evidence should an abuse victim later try to obtain a protection order or custody of the children.

Many abuse survivors have benefited from mandatory prosecution and arrest laws. However, not all couple relationships are the same and some experts contend that mandatory reporting and prosecution laws violate an abuse survivor's freedom of choice. Linda Mills, a legal scholar, social worker, and herself a domestic violence survivor, believes that the system currently fails to listen to survivors, takes away their decision-making power, and underestimates their ability to protect themselves. Although survivors want the abuse to stop, they often do not want to put their spouse in jail. Some do not want to cause their abuser to have a criminal record. Others depend on the wages the abuser brings home. Still others fear that sending the abuser to jail will just make things worse.

This fear that jailing the abuser will make things worse is well founded. The experience of an abuse victim named Lisa is not uncommon: After Lisa's abusive ex-husband was released from prison, he drove 150 miles, broke in to her house, and killed her.

Self-defense or murder?

Men who kill their wives are frequently considered to commit murder during a fit of anger or jealousy, which is viewed by the law as a crime of passion. A crime of passion carries a lesser sentence than murder does, thus abusive men who kill their partners often receive shorter sentences than do those who have killed a stranger.

By contrast, women who kill their abusive partners in self-defense often receive harsh sentences. Jan Berliner Statman notes, "There is a serious form of gender bias in the laws of self-defense, which were originally designed to deal with barroom brawls between two men of equal strength, not between life and death battles between a 225-pound man and a 110-pound woman."[54] While a battered woman's partner can beat her to death with his fists, she must find another way to defend herself and overpower her assailant physically. Kay Bartlett, writing for the *Los Angeles Times*, gives the following example: "A woman who decides to use a gun cannot risk a violent husband disarming her, so she may start shooting while he is asleep, has his back turned, or is drunk."[55] Shooting an unarmed person usually brings a state's most serious charge, such as aggravated murder. In addition, the battered woman sometimes continues shooting long after her abuser is dead. According to Lenore Walker, a well-known expert on domestic violence, "[Battered women] are so afraid, feel so powerless, and believe [their abuser] is omnipotent and about to rise up at any moment and beat them, that they keep shooting even when it would be clear to most people that the first bullet has killed."[56] Lacking the understanding of the dynamics of domestic violence, juries can find it hard to believe a battered woman's claim that she was in danger of being killed or severely beaten and that killing her partner was self-defense.

Prosecution of abusers

In general, then, although the legal system is supposed to support and protect victims of domestic violence, as Lundy Bancroft notes, "courts reserve a special skepticism

toward women who complain of abuse by a partner."[57]
Studies show that it is harder to convince judges and juries
to convict in abuse cases. Judges and juries appear preju-
diced against women who complain of abuse and harbor
misconceptions about what type of man would abuse his
wife. Thus, it is rare for an abuser to spend time in jail unless he is on his third or fourth conviction.

Another factor in the legal system's failure to address
domestic violence is that such cases often are tried in civil
rather than criminal courts, and civil court judges do not
always have easy access to, nor do they necessarily consider, the criminal records of abusers. For example, a
Massachusetts municipal judge granted Kristin the restraining order she sought, but then turned her abuser,
Michael, loose. Within a month, Michael killed Kristin.
What the judge did not know when he released Michael

*Battered women who
kill their abusers with a
firearm often receive
harsher sentences than
male abusers who kill
their partners during a
fit of rage.*

was that Michael had a criminal record of violent crimes against women and was on probation for attacking a previous girlfriend. Samuel Zoll, chief justice of the Massachusetts district courts, explained, "You can't mix civil and criminal records."[58]

Abuser programs

One way of addressing domestic violence is to get abusers to participate in programs designed to help them change their behavior. Just how much good such programs do, however, is a matter of debate among domestic violence experts. For example, after fifteen years of working with abusive men, Lundy Bancroft has come to the conclusion that it is possible for an abuser to change, but it takes a lot of work and most men find it easier to remain abusive. In fact, experts find that, since abusers are rewarded for their abuse, getting what they want when they want it, there is little incentive for them to change. In Bancroft's experience, "The men who make significant progress in my program are the ones who know that their partners will definitely leave them unless they change, and the ones on probation who have a tough probation officer who demands that they really confront their abusiveness."[59]

Experts agree that without consequences, most abusers have no reason to change. The challenge remains how to hold abusers accountable for their actions while protecting their victims from retaliation.

4

Elder Abuse

OF ALL THE forms of family violence, elder abuse has historically received the least attention. As a result, experts in the field have yet to reach a consensus on definitions of elder abuse. The authors of *Family Violence Across the Lifespan* note, "With little agreement on who should care for elders and how they should be cared for, it should come as no surprise that there is little agreement on how elder abuse should be defined."[60] Researchers also are still studying the factors that contribute to and are important in preventing elder abuse. Finally, experts are struggling with the issue of an individual's right to choose versus the state's obligation to protect older adults.

The nature of abuse

Elders suffer from the same types of abuse as other victims of family violence. They may be physically, sexually, and emotionally abused at the hands of their relatives or caregivers. Elders may also suffer from neglect, but the issues are more complex than they are for younger people. The authors of *Family Violence Across the Lifespan* explain:

> There are no clear norms or moral rules about who is responsible for elder care. Adult children are not legally required to help an elder parent in need; moreover, approximately 20 percent of elders are childless. Because there are no agreed-on moral or legal standards concerning responsibility for elders, therefore, it is difficult to know who should be held accountable for their care or neglect.[61]

When there is a relative or caregiver who has taken responsibility for caring for an older adult, it is easier to determine if neglect is taking place. Neglect occurs when abusers do not provide for the basic needs of their victims. This can include refusal to provide food, water, shelter, comfort, or medical care. For older adults, neglect can also include failure to manage the elder's money or property appropriately.

Sometimes, the neglect is unintentional. For example, caregivers who do not understand the type of care an elder needs can cause an elder to be neglected. In addition, caregivers who are unable to provide needed care, such as a spouse who is in ill health herself, can also contribute to neglect. The Walkinses are an example of a couple struggling with this situation. Mr. Walkins is eighty-one years old and unable to walk. He has infected bedsores because he spends too much time in bed. Mrs. Walkins is seventy-nine years old and willingly cares for her husband. She is in good health but is too small and frail to lift her husband from his bed into his wheelchair. Her eyesight is also so poor that she cannot see his bedsores well enough to treat them properly. In short, although willing, Mrs. Walkins is unable to provide her husband with the care he needs.

Self-neglect

Like the Walkinses, most elders remain responsible for their own care, and some are unable to care for themselves properly. Some professionals in the field include such self-neglect among the types of elder abuse. Self-neglect occurs when an elder's behavior threatens his or her health and safety. According to the National Center on Elder Abuse, self-neglect generally shows itself in an elderly person's "refusal or failure to provide himself/herself with adequate food, water, clothing, shelter, personal hygiene, medication (when indicated), and safety precautions."[62]

In one study of reported elder abuse cases, 42 percent of the cases involved self-neglect. However, not all experts agree that self-neglect should be considered abuse. Cer-

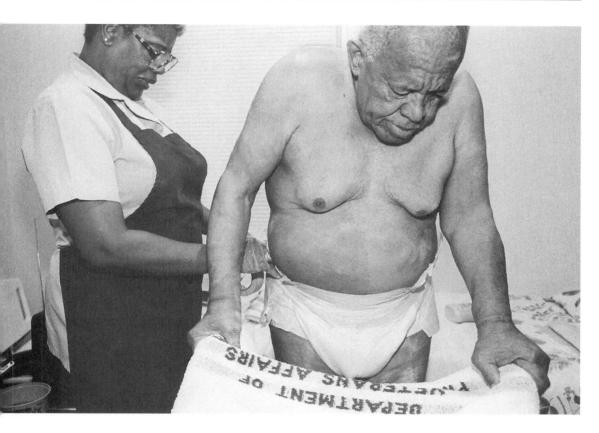

tainly self-neglect puts an elder in danger, but it does not involve a victim-abuser relationship between two people. In addition, self-neglect rests on issues of personal competency that are controversial among professionals, relatives of older adults, and elders themselves. In other words, there is a conflict between an elder's right as an adult to make decisions for him- or herself and the reality that the elder may no longer understand the consequences of his or her actions.

This elderly man moved in with his grandson's family once he found it too difficult to care for himself. Like children, the elderly cannot defend themselves against abuse.

Financial abuse

There is no controversy, however, about including financial abuse among the forms of elder abuse. Financial abuse occurs when someone uses the elder's money or property improperly. Cashing an older person's checks, stealing an older person's money or possessions, or tricking an

Socially isolated elders are highly susceptible to financial abuse. Swindlers devise elaborate schemes in order to defraud elderly people out of their savings.

elder into signing documents that give the abuser power over the elder's money or property are all examples of financial abuse. The *Oregonian* ran a story in spring 2003 about a seventy-eight-year-old victim of financial abuse. According to the news story, the woman's nephew "coerced her into taking out a $90,000 mortgage on her house. He took her to the mortgage company and said, 'Sign here, sign here, sign here.' The nephew took $40,000 to pay off his credit cards and the rest in cash for cars and fun."[63] A volunteer from Elder Safe, an organization dedicated to protecting senior citizens, helped the woman go to court and evict her nephew. Although she was forced to sell her house, she was not left destitute. Another eighty-eight-year-old woman was not so lucky.

Her caregiver stole over $41,000, leaving the woman bankrupt, unable to pay for her own care, and forced to move out of her own home.

No matter how one defines elder abuse, it is a large problem. Over 1 million adults over the age of sixty are victims of elder abuse, although some experts estimate the number may be much higher. In addition, the problem is growing. As Rosalie S. Wolf and Karl A. Pillemer, well-known researchers in the field of elder abuse, observe, "Professionals who work with the elderly have pointed out that many problems of the elderly, including abuse and neglect by family members, can be expected to increase, simply because of the growth in the numbers of the aged."[64] Already the number of reported cases of elder abuse more than doubled between 1986 and 1996 and grew another third between 1996 and the year 2000. Although some of the increase may be due to an increased awareness and reporting of abuse, the growing population of elders is also a factor.

Who is at risk?

Because there is no consistent definition of elder abuse, it is difficult to say who is at risk of being abused. However, some patterns are starting to emerge. Most elder abuse victims seem to live in the community rather than in institutions. Thus, they most often are abused by members of their own family. Typically the abuser is the victim's spouse or an adult child who lives with the victim. Studies have also found that elders over seventy-five years old are in the most danger of suffering from elder abuse. Elder abuse seems to occur at all levels of society and among all ethnic and racial groups.

Regardless of who is at risk, social isolation appears to increase the chances that an elder will be abused. Isolation, experts say, tends to contribute to a decline in one's ability to think and make decisions. This makes isolated elders more vulnerable to manipulation and abuse by others. Isolation can also be a side effect of abuse. The abuser often purposely isolates the victim to prevent others from learning about the abuse. That isolation serves to make

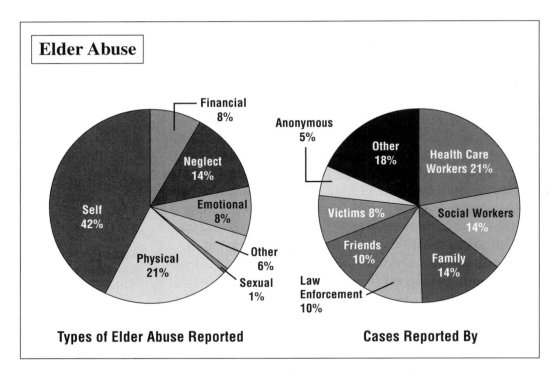

Elder Abuse

Financial 8%
Neglect 14%
Self 42%
Emotional 8%
Physical 21%
Other 6%
Sexual 1%

Anonymous 5%
Other 18%
Health Care Workers 21%
Victims 8%
Social Workers 14%
Friends 10%
Family 14%
Law Enforcement 10%

Types of Elder Abuse Reported

Cases Reported By

the elder even more dependent the abuser, creating a vicious cycle.

A portrait of the abuser

The isolation of the victim is something elder abuse shares with other forms of family violence. Unlike child abuse and domestic violence, however, the abuse does not seem to be learned behavior. Abused children, for example, do not usually later on abuse their elderly parents. Indeed, it is the elder's prior experience that is a predictor of abuse. Those who have been abused in the past are in more danger of suffering from elder abuse.

It is the long-term dynamics of the relationship between caregiver and older adult that seem to play an important role. Adult children who abuse their parents mostly are children who live with and depend on their parents for financial or other support. It appears that these adult children have trouble making it in society on their own. They may use drugs or alcohol. They may have trouble finding and keeping jobs. They may even have a history of arrest. These children have problems of their own.

Myrna Reis's study of the factors that underlie elder abuse in Canada led her to conclude that "the typical abuse case is characterized by (1) a troubled caregiver who has difficulty getting along with others and (2) a situation in which the care recipient has been abused in the past and in which there is inadequate social support."[65]

Abuse goes undetected

Among elders it is even more likely that abuse will go undetected. Unlike children who go to school or working-age adults, elders may be less mobile and therefore leave their homes infrequently, making it harder for someone to see or notice the abuse.

Even among elders who are not isolated, abuse can go undetected. Dr. Mark S. Lachs, a physician at Yale University's School of Medicine, notes,

> Older adults have a higher burden of chronic disease than younger adults. If a patient has a hip fracture for example, it is very easy to ascribe that injury to osteoporosis and a fall when in fact it may have resulted from physical violence. . . . There is a tendency to simply chalk off many of the signs and symptoms of elder abuse to "just getting old."[66]

Even extreme cases of abuse may go undetected for a long period. The *Seattle Times* reported on the case of Mac, an eighty-two-year-old man who was found locked in his filthy, hot room, without water or ventilation, and wearing a garbage bag as a diaper. According to the report, "His neighbors had heard him call for help, repeatedly, but because he had Alzheimer's disease, they figured it was normal and didn't want to interfere."[67]

Finally, elders may react to abuse the way survivors of other types of family violence do. Many deliberately do not seek out elder abuse services. According to Rosalie Wolf, former president of the National Committee for the Prevention of Elder Abuse, "Reports of elder abuse are often met with disbelief. People just don't think it happens. It's hidden. Elders do not talk about it. They often deny that it occurred; they feel ashamed, embarrassed, and humiliated."[68] In addition, some elders do not want to create conflict in the family or community. Many choose not to report their abuse if it means sending a child, spouse, or other loved one to jail.

Adult Protective Services

Because the elderly are less mobile than younger people, elder abuse is more likely to go undetected than other types of abuse.

In an effort to get help to abused elders, every state has passed some form of elder abuse reporting law. These laws vary from state to state. In most states, the Adult Protective Services (APS) program receives reports and complaints of elder abuse. Each agency reviews and investigates all reports of elder abuse among adults living in their own homes or apartments or with family or friends. For the over

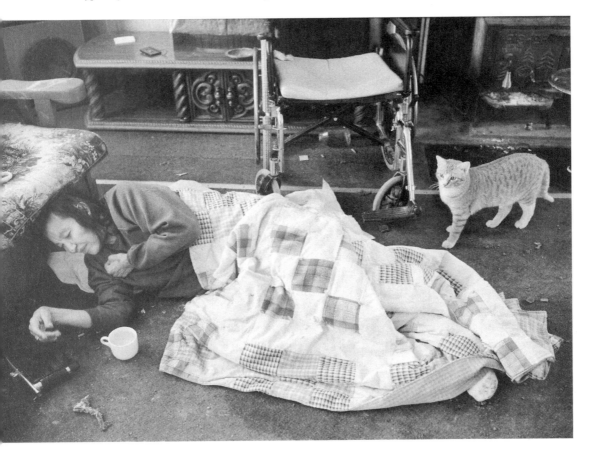

50 percent of cases that are confirmed, APS workers try to coordinate health and social services to address the problem. Adult Protective Services also works with the courts and law enforcement agencies as needed. The main goal of most state APS programs is to help elders and other vulnerable adults live independently at home while keeping them safe from abuse.

Experts note, however, that APS programs have problems, since they are based on invalid stereotypes. When these programs were developed elders were seen as incapable and vulnerable adults needing protection, while abusers were seen as well-meaning but overburdened daughters trying to care for their elderly parents. Elder abuse itself, then, was stereotyped as being like child abuse, with elders entering their second childhood and adults failing to protect them. Accordingly, Adult Protective Services programs were modeled after Child Protective Services.

Caregiver stress?

In addition to the stereotyping there were other problems with the Adult Protective Services model. One such problem was the assumption that the stress of caregiving caused elder abuse. It is true that caring for an older adult can be stressful. The elder may need lots of help with bathing, eating, dressing, and fetching items. Some elders can also be demanding because of chronic pain or memory loss. The assumption was that under stress caregivers lost control and abused the elder they were caring for. Research, however, has shown this is not the case. Neither caregiver stress nor demanding elders are the cause of elder abuse. Georgia J. Anetzberger sums up the research when she says, "Caregiving is not the primary cause of elder abuse. Rather, it is a context for interaction in which abuse can occur."[69] In other words, caregiving puts the victim and abuser in close contact and can provide a caregiver who is inclined to abuse the opportunity to do so.

Undue influence

Caregiving can also provide an opening for what experts call undue influence. Undue influence occurs when what one person wants is substituted for the desires of another. Fraud, threats, and other types of pressure can be applied to get the elder to do what the person in control wants. Both family members and outsiders can be guilty of exercising undue influence. In either case, the result can be the caregiver ending up controlling and manipulating the elder he or she is caring for. In the words of Mary Joy Quinn,

> We have marveled at the actions of seemingly competent and capable elders who have given away major assets under dumbfounding circumstances. We have puzzled over situations in which elders have given valuable personal items or money to caregivers or to only one family member. Some elders seem to turn away from family members and place all their trust in virtual strangers. Often, after the elder dies, the will is filed and the stranger is the only beneficiary.[70]

Margaret Singer, an expert on undue influence, has found a pattern used by abusers who practice undue influence. The pattern is similar to the manipulation and isolation strategies used by perpetrators of domestic violence. The abuser first courts and gains the trust of the elder. Once the elder trusts the abuser, the abuser works to isolate the elder and make him or her dependent on the abuser. Singer explains,

> [The elder] is told that no one but the caregiver is concerned with the elder. All others, including professionals, are portrayed as wanting to take advantage of the elder or wanting to put her in a nursing home or abandon her. Even though the caregiver [abuser] has engineered the isolation and methodically kept friends and family away, the caregiver [abuser] tells the victim that others do not care and have abandoned the elder. Finally the victim becomes fearful and recognizes her vulnerability. At that point, the victim is easily manipulated into financial and material abuse.[71]

One example of such manipulation is the case of a retired schoolteacher who, after she had a mild stroke, fell

This nursing home worker received a prison sentence for felony elder abuse. Abusive caregivers often attempt to control the behavior of their victims.

victim to the caregiver who was hired to help her. The caregiver characterized small medical problems as big ones, insisting the elder stay in bed to rest. The caregiver removed the clock, calendar, television, and radio so that the woman had no sense of time. In addition, the caregiver overdosed her charge with drugs and underfed her so that she was always weak and sleepy. When friends called on the phone or came to the house, the caregiver told them the woman was too sick to receive visitors. Once the elder

Some elderly victims suffer years of abuse at the hands of a spouse. Those that do seek help often find fewer resources available to them than those offered to younger victims.

was isolated and dependent, the caregiver brought in a lawyer and had the elder change her will to benefit the caregiver.

Domestic violence grown old

Such isolation and manipulation is often a familiar pattern for many victims. It is now accepted among experts that a good portion of elder abuse is domestic violence grown old. That is, these victims are elders who continue to suffer from abuse by an aging spouse or partner. The abuser, who over the years has expected all his needs to be met by his partner, may now face a situation where his partner is ill and unable to meet those needs. One elderly abuser, for example, claimed that his wife had ruined his later years by having a stroke. In his view, she was supposed to be waiting on him and instead he was taking care of her. He responded to her needs only when he felt like it and held a pillow over her face whenever she fussed too much.

Victims of this sort of elder abuse are at a disadvantage. There are few shelters that provide services to elders. In addition, many APS workers mistakenly provide support for the abuser. They listen to the abuser talk about the burden of caring for his partner and worry about caregiver stress. Unknowingly, they reinforce the abuser's sense that his partner is at fault, confirming in his mind that his partner's behavior is to blame.

A tough spot

Adult Protective Services workers dealing with such cases find themselves in a tough spot. Caseworkers try to coordinate services and help elder abuse victims without adequate knowledge of what does or does not work. According to the authors of *Family Violence Across the Lifespan*, "It is not uncommon for victims to receive services that they do not need, insufficient services, or even refusal by agency personnel to provide services requested."[72]

At the heart of the problem is the original modeling of Adult Protective Services after Child Protective Services. Experts point out, for example, that treating adults like children can result in depriving them of their civil rights. While authorities can assume parental responsibility for an abused child and make decisions regarding his or her welfare, they can make decisions for elders only if they are judged incapable of making their own decisions.

Given such problems, Rosalie S. Wolf states, "New findings on the prevalence of spouse abuse in the elderly

An elderly woman with dementia is hospitalized. Elders with dementia are frequent targets of abuse as a result of their impaired decision-making abilities.

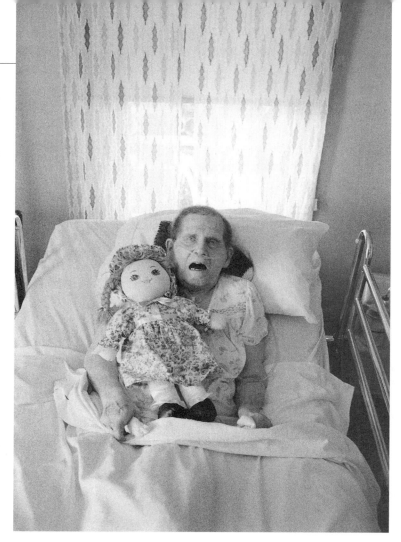

populations suggested that the domestic violence model might be a better fit."[73] There is still much to learn about elder abuse. In the meantime, current efforts to prevent elder abuse focus on educating the public and professionals about the problem and about possible responses. Changes are also occurring within social services, law enforcement, and the courts, but the field is still hampered by the lack of consistent definitions of elder abuse and by the fact that like all forms of family violence, much of it remains hidden.

5

Protecting Families

As THE TERM implies, family violence affects the entire family. Yet experts are only beginning to acknowledge this, and most efforts to address abuse have not focused on the whole family. As a result, laws designed to prevent child abuse fail to take into account the possible presence of domestic violence in the family. For their part, advocates trying to prevent domestic violence often have not considered the effect of their efforts on other family members.

Failure-to-protect laws

One example of well-intended efforts gone awry is failure-to-protect laws. These laws, which are designed to combat child abuse, can have a severe impact on victims of domestic violence.

As the name implies, failure-to-protect laws impose penalties on a parent who does not protect his or her child from abuse. The rationale is that good parents will do whatever is necessary to prevent abuse. Under these laws, if a parent leaves a child alone with a known abuser, is there when the child is abused and does not stop the abuse, or does not take an injured child to get medical care, the parent can be considered unfit and lose his or her children permanently.

Removing the child from the situation, throwing the abuser out of the house, or reporting the abuse all meet the requirement that a parent is protecting his or her child. Yet when domestic violence is also present, the nonabusive parent may not be able to take any of these actions. The nonviolent parent may not interfere with the abuse for fear of making things worse. She may not report the abuse because she is afraid that the abuser will retaliate with greater violence. The abused parent may also decide that leaving the abuser is more dangerous than staying.

The majority of states now have failure-to-protect laws on their books. Very few of these laws allow the courts to consider evidence that attempts by the nonviolent parent to protect the child would have resulted in additional injury to the nonviolent parent or the child. Low-income abused parents are in an especially difficult spot. If they stay with the abuser, they risk losing custody of their children because they cannot stop the abuse. If they leave, they risk losing custody of their children because they do not have the money to provide adequate food and shelter.

Martha A. Matthews, a lawyer at the National Center for Youth Law in San Francisco, notes,

> The underlying assumption on which these laws are based . . . fails to recognize that many battered parents lack resources to immediately escape from violent situations and feed, clothe, and house their children on their own; that attempts to escape a violent home may actually increase the battered parent's and the children's risk of being injured or killed; and that battered parents may, to protect their own and their children's lives in the long term, be compelled to endure abuse until they can develop a safe and effective plan to leave the violent situation.[74]

Child custody and visitation

Failure-to-protect laws are not the only laws with good intentions that can harm families suffering from family violence. Child custody and visitation rulings can also place domestic violence survivors and abused children in danger of further abuse. Since the 1970s, courts have tried to award divorced parents joint custody of their children. Special efforts have been made to encourage fathers to remain involved in the lives of their children.

In cases of child abuse, however, joint custody gives the abuser continued access to his or her victim. In cases of domestic violence, the abuser can use joint custody or visi-

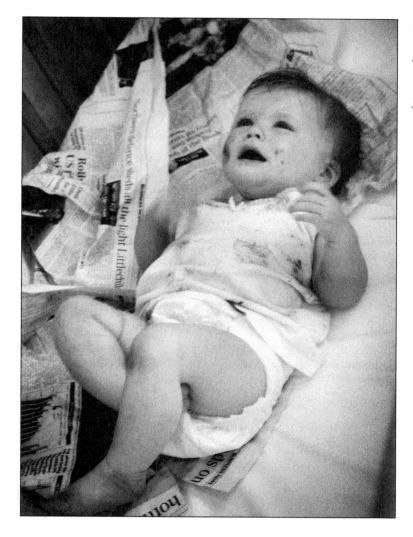

Divorce court rulings that award visitation or joint-custody rights to abusers can subject abused children to further violence.

tation as a tool to remain in contact with or threaten the abused partner. In one study, one-fourth of the women reported that they had received threats against their lives during visitation.

Given the potential danger, more than half the states now have laws that require that domestic violence be considered when courts grant child custody and visitation rights. However, common practices and lack of knowledge about the reality of family violence continue to influence courts' decisions.

Friendly parent laws

One such common practice is dictated by what are known as friendly parent laws, another example of laws that can unintentionally harm the very people they are meant to help. Friendly parent laws dictate that in divorce cases the court considers which parent is most willing to share custody in deciding where the children will actually live. The rationale for such laws is that the parent who is willing to share custody most likely has the best interests of the children at heart. As a result, the court will frequently give this parent custody of the children.

Experts note that such laws do not consider that in cases where child abuse is involved, the abuser may be willing to share custody while the other parent is not. The nonviolent parent may argue that, for the safety of the child, the child should have no further contact with the abusing parent. To many judges this is seen as not cooperating with the court.

In divorce cases, the judge often awards child custody to the parent most willing to share custody with the other. In this way, abusive parents sometimes win custody battles.

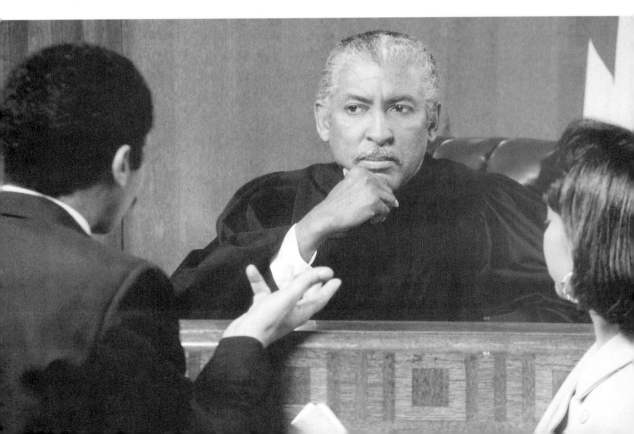

In some cases these judges will give the abuser full custody of the child he or she has been abusing. Lundy Bancroft, an expert on abusive men, is scornful of this practice: "The treatment that protective mothers so often receive at the hands of family courts is among the most shameful secrets of modern jurisprudence. This is the only social institution that I am aware of that so frequently forbids mothers to protect their children from abuse."[75]

Supervised visitation

Even when the nonviolent parent is given custody of the child, the abuser is often given visitation rights. Visitation rights in such cases can put both the child and the abused parent in danger by giving the abuser continued contact with his or her victims. For example, Christopher used his visitation time to verbally and physically attack his ex-wife Dawn. More than a year after their divorce, while on a visit with his daughter, Christopher dragged Dawn from her apartment and tried to kill her. A year later, Christopher was still writing her threatening letters from jail stating, "You'll never keep me from [our daughter]" and "You're going to have to deal with me in life sometime down the road."[76]

To address this problem, many states are passing new laws that require the courts to consider the safety of both the child and the abused parent when granting visitation rights. Courts see supervised visitation as a way of addressing some of the safety issues. In supervised visitation, someone else must be present to protect the child. This also allays the fears of the nonviolent parent. In the words of a parent who uses the YMCA Visitation Center in Springfield, Massachusetts, "It gives me peace of mind to know that my kids are safe. He can't just take them. He can't hit them."[77]

Although the use of supervised visitation is promising, the services are not free, and many families cannot afford to pay for them. In addition, there are few supervised visitation centers available. Thus, many nonviolent parents are forced to provide supervision themselves or rely on family or friends. Carol, whose ex-husband is only allowed to see his children in her home under her supervision because of his violent behavior, finds herself in such a bind:

> He comes into her apartment every Sunday afternoon, watches her TV, becomes unruly and breaks her furniture, and eats all the food she bought on her small salary, leaving the family to go hungry the rest of the week. Carol is afraid to complain to the court for fear a new hearing will somehow award this dangerous man unsupervised visitation rights.[78]

To prevent similar situations, the American Bar Association (ABA) recommends that the abuser be required to pay the cost of supervised visitations. In addition, some states are creating state-run supervised visitation centers. Where they exist, these visitation centers have been well received.

Stable parent

Just as courts tend to favor the parent willing to share custody, they also favor the parent who appears more stable and earns a higher income when they assign custody. The logic is that the more stable and wealthier parent will be better able to meet the needs of the children. Although this can be a valid assumption in many divorce cases, it does not necessarily hold true for families suffering from domestic violence.

A newly escaped abused wife frequently appears less stable than her violent partner does. She may have left everything she owned behind when she escaped; she may be moving from place to place to keep her abuser from discovering where she and her children live; she may still be looking for work, or have an uneven employment history if her abuser forced her to quit working while they were together.

On the other hand, the violent parent may well have a history of steady employment. He may be living in the family house. He may even have remarried. The violent parent may also be able to convince the judge that his wife abandoned the children if she left them behind or that she kidnapped the children if she took them with her.

Marlon Brando's son Christian is reunited with his mother after the court granted her visitation rights. In cases of abuse, the court may mandate that such visits be supervised.

The violent partner may also appear in control in court, while his victim may still be traumatized from the abuse. Abused parents can appear unstable, nervous, and angry. They may be intimidated and flustered by the presence of their abuser. In short, the violent parent may appear more stable and gain custody as a result. Even judges who know that the nonviolent parent is competent can be fooled. For example, one abused wife was so intimidated by her husband in the hallway before entering court that she was unable to function despite the fact that she was an experienced trial lawyer herself. Although she had successfully argued cases before the same judge, he granted her husband full custody of the children. The judge explained to the woman's lawyer that he based his decision on the fact that the wife was not acting like herself. In her agitated state, the judge felt it would be in her best interest to give her "relief from childcare for a while so she could pull herself together."[79]

This judge is not alone in his lack of understanding of the dynamics of family violence. The ABA now recommends that state laws go beyond requiring courts to consider the presence of domestic violence when ruling on child custody cases. The ABA wants states to pass laws requiring courts to favor granting child custody to the nonviolent parent. Several states have passed such laws. Others require that courts consider both the safety of the child and the abused parent when making custody decisions.

Need for collaboration

With increased recognition that multiple forms of violence can exist within a family, experts are calling for coordination between agencies dealing with child abuse, domestic violence, and elder abuse. Such coordination is growing but still rare. The case of a family in Rhode Island is more typical: "A battered woman appeared at a hospital emergency room with her bruised toddler. None of the doctors or nurses who treated the mother examined the child, and after the woman was patched up, no one thought to notify Child Protective Services. Nine months after the mother's visit to the ER, the baby was killed by the same violent boyfriend who had been beating the mother."[80]

Janet Carter, of the Family Violence Fund in San Francisco, and Susan Kelly, of the Families First program in Lansing, Michigan, note, "Historically, domestic violence service programs and the child welfare system have often worked with the same families but did not work together to create safe, coordinated, and effective responses for family violence."[81] For example, when CPS workers investigate reports of child abuse, they typically check all the children for signs of abuse but do not follow up on evidence of domestic violence. Similarly, police responding to domestic violence calls typically focus on the adults involved and sometimes ignore the children. Domestic violence shelters focus on meeting the many needs of abused women and only recently have started to provide more than basic child care and needed medical care for their children.

Although the need for collaboration is increasingly being recognized, working across fields can be challenging. Workers in each field have their own way of doing things. Professionals in one field often do not trust the way professionals in related fields work. For example, the relationship between child welfare workers and domestic violence service workers has traditionally been difficult at best. Janet Carter and Susan Kelly note, "Mistrust was common on both sides. Non-cooperation the rule."[82]

Some domestic violence workers do not trust child abuse workers because they have the legal authority to impose decisions on families. Many domestic violence workers also

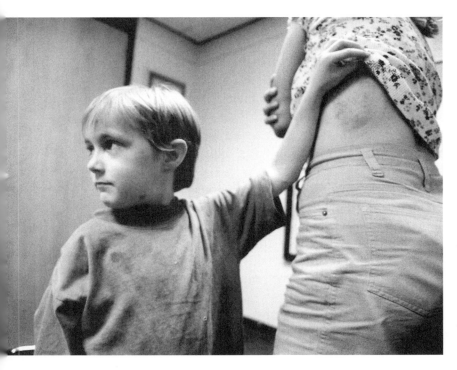

A boy shows police the bruises his mother received from her boyfriend. In such domestic violence cases, police frequently fail to check the children for signs of abuse.

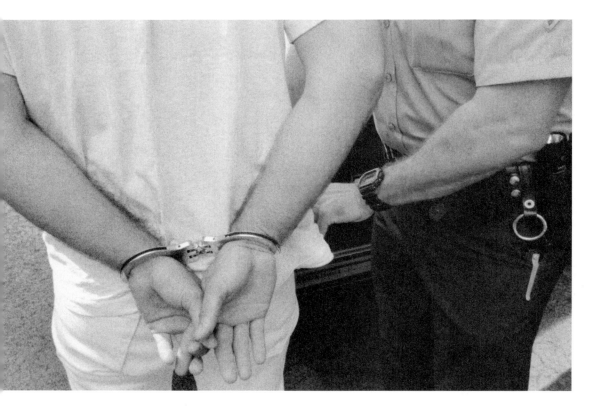

believe that the child protection system revictimizes abused mothers. This is especially the case when the system takes away an abused mother's children after accusing her of failing to protect them. Finally, according to Carter and Kelly, "Many battered women's advocates fear family preservation means encouraging women to stay with their batterers."[83]

For their part, child protection workers are equally suspicious of domestic violence workers. They think that domestic violence workers focus on abused women and regard their well-being as more important than the welfare of their children. They accuse domestic violence workers of refusing to acknowledge and deal with the fact that women, not just men, abuse and neglect children as well. Finally, some child abuse workers do not trust domestic violence workers because they allow women and children to return home to dangerous situations.

Working together

Interdisciplinary approaches and response team are becoming more common, however. Child abuse, domestic violence, and elder abuse experts are training each other on how to respond to and help all members of a family. Armed with this knowledge, abuse prevention workers are better able to help all family members regardless of the type of abuse. Sometimes this means that workers learn to recognize the signs of all types of family violence and can get help from experts in the other fields when needed. Other times experts from each field work together as a team.

The Massachusetts Department of Social Services developed the first systemwide effort to include both domestic violence and child abuse expertise when making decisions regarding a family. Protection of abused children is combined with services for their abused mothers. The agency's Domestic Violence Unit has experienced domestic violence workers working in the same office as child protection workers. By working together in close proximity, domestic violence workers learn about the problems of trying to prevent child abuse and child protection workers gain assistance with domestic violence problems in the families they work with. The domestic violence workers also provide a link between Child Protective Services and community domestic violence programs that both groups trust.

According to the authors of *Family Violence: Emerging Programs for Battered Mothers and Their Children*, the Massachusetts program

> has increased the ability of Department of Social Services staff to recognize domestic violence in their cases, reduced unnecessary out-of-home placement of children, and increased cooperation between battered women's advocates and child protection workers. . . . The program also appears to have brought a new perspective to the Department of Social Services, allowing staff to view care in the context of a violent family as opposed to a single incident.[84]

Expanding services

Collaboration across fields has not only changed the way that abuse prevention workers look at family violence but has resulted in child abuse, elder abuse, and domestic violence programs altering their services to better address the needs of the whole family. One of the organizations that has expanded its services in this way is the Women's Center and Shelter of Greater Pittsburgh (WC&S). The WC&S closely coordinates services for both child and adult survivors of abuse. For example, counseling services are provided for both abused women and their children. Child and adult counselors then work together to ensure that the needs of both mother and child are met.

The WC&S also runs a family advocacy program in collaboration with Children and Youth Services. Among other activities, experts on domestic violence train all Children and Youth Services workers and are available to help these workers with individual cases in which families are trying to cope with both child abuse and domestic violence. By developing a broad collaboration, the WC&S is at the center of a web of community services. It receives referrals from schools, doctors, therapists, Children and Youth Ser-

Some victims of family violence find comfort in discussing their problems with friends or former abuse victims.

vices, and the community. Its links to diverse community services allow help to be coordinated for families suffering from family violence.

In addition to collaborations between workers trying to prevent different forms of family violence, collaborations are also expanding to include disciplines whose focus is not family violence. For example, the Family Violence and Sexual Assault Unit in Philadelphia brings together lawyers, victims' advocates, police officers, and the district attorney so that social services and prosecution can be woven together to best support the family.

Domestic violence hotlines are just one of many social services offered that attempt to help deal with the complex and far-reaching problem of family violence.

Death review teams

One of the most powerful collaborations currently operating are death review teams. Child death review teams and domestic violence review teams bring together members of many disciplines, including health, mental health, social services, law enforcement, criminal justice, and education. Death review teams share information across disciplines to create a picture of what happened in cases where a person died as a result of family violence. Often, each group has different information through previous contacts with the murder victim, but no one had a clear enough understanding to prevent the death. According to the U.S. Advisory Board on Child Abuse and Neglect,

> It is not unusual for law enforcement to be aware of domestic violence problems in a family, for Child Protective Services to know about an allegation of molestation against the mother's boyfriend, and for public health nurses to be tracking an infant in the home suffering from malnutrition or failure to thrive. Yet more often than not, none of this information is seen in its entirety by any one professional.[85]

Death review teams pass the results of their findings on to law enforcement to prosecute the abuser when appropriate. Death review teams also identify areas where systems break down and fail to protect abuse victims, look for clues on how to improve existing systems, and identify gaps where prevention programs are needed. Child and domestic violence death review teams also provide a forum for representatives of many disciplines to come together and share approaches to preventing family violence. This opportunity to break down barriers between disciplines helps set the stage for more coordinated action to prevent family violence.

What works?

There is still a great deal experts do not know about family violence. Many of the common patterns of family violence are known, but the best way to intervene to prevent such violence is still not clear. There is controversy about whether a victim has the right to choose who he or she lives with or whether the government is obligated to protect an abuse victim from further abuse. Advocates are still trying to learn how to help without putting survivors in further danger. There is still work to be done before the public and professionals fully understand the dynamics of family violence.

Collaborations across fields help break down some of the false assumptions. Collaboration can also help coordinate prevention efforts to best serve all members of a family suffering from family violence. For real progress to be made, however, experts believe that the silence surrounding family violence needs to be broken.

Dr. Timmen L. Cermak notes, "Silence is deadly. The universal human impulse is to deny abuse, whether you perpetrated it or suffered it. But the price of silence and denial is far too great. . . . Victims of abuse must find the courage to speak truthfully about their experiences. One of the primary sources of their courage is our willingness to listen."[86] Suzanne, a survivor of child abuse, agrees: "Child abuse—be it physical, sexual, or emotional—thrives in secret. As long as the perpetrators feel their actions will go unacknowledged and undetected, they will persist. They won't seek help. And their victims will remain without a voice."[87]

Notes

Introduction

1. Quoted in Jeffrey Artenstein, *Runaways: In Their Own Words: Kids Talking About Living on the Streets.* New York: Tom Doherty Associates, 1990, p. 129.

2. Quoted in Leslie A. Cantrell, *Into the Light: A Guide for Battered Women.* Edmonds, WA: Charles Franklin Press, 1986, p. 14.

3. American Psychological Association Presidential Task Force on Violence and the Family, *Violence and the Family.* Washington, DC: American Psychological Association, 1996, p. 6.

4. Quoted in Barbara Cottrell, *Parent Abuse: The Abuse of Parents by Their Teenage Children.* Ottawa, Canada: National Clearinghouse on Family Violence, Family Violence Prevention Unit, Health Canada, 2001, p. 24.

Chapter 1: Family Violence and Its Impact

5. Quoted in Gertrude J. Williams and John Money, eds., *Traumatic Abuse and Neglect of Children at Home.* Baltimore, MD: Johns Hopkins University Press, 1980, pp. 23–24.

6. Quoted in Liz Claiborne Women's Work, *A Parent's Guide to Teen Dating Violence: 10 Questions to Start the Conversation*, New York: Liz Claiborne, Inc., 2001, p. 12. www.lizclaiborne.com/lizinc/lizworks/women.

7. Quoted in Artenstein, *Runaways*, p. 2.

8. Quoted in Williams and Money, *Traumatic Abuse and Neglect of Children at Home*, pp. 71–72.

9. Quoted in Liz Claiborne Women's Work, *What you*

Need to Know About Dating Violence: A Teen's Handbook, New York: Liz Claiborne, Inc., 2000, p. 21. www.lizclaiborne. com/lizinc/lizworks/women.

10. Quoted in Suzanne Somers, *Wednesday's Children: Adult Survivors of Abuse Speak Out.* New York: Jove/Healing Vision, 1993, p. 199.

11. Quoted in Jan Berliner Statman, *The Battered Woman's Survival Guide: Breaking the Cycle.* Dallas: Taylor, 1990, p. 54.

12. Quoted in Statman, *The Battered Woman's Survival Guide*, p. 67.

13. Quoted in Statman, *The Battered Woman's Survival Guide*, p. 54.

14. Quoted in Cantrell, *Into the Light*, p. 6.

15. Quoted in Somers, *Wednesday's Children*, p. 149.

16. Quoted in Cantrell, *Into the Light*, p. 8.

17. Quoted in Cantrell, *Into the Light*, p. 6.

18. Quoted in Somers, *Wednesday's Children*, p. 108.

19. Quoted in Statman, *The Battered Woman's Survival Guide*, pp. 64–65.

20. Quoted in Statman, *The Battered Woman's Survival Guide*, p. 70.

21. Quoted in Somers, *Wednesday's Children*, p. 50.

22. Quoted in Williams and Money, *Traumatic Abuse and Neglect of Children at Home*, p. 21.

23. Quoted in Somers, *Wednesday's Children*, pp. 82–83.

24. Quoted in Somers, *Wednesday's Children*, p. 128.

25. Quoted in Somers, *Wednesday's Children*, p. 170.

26. American Psychological Association, "Facts About Family Violence," 2003. www.apa.org/releases/facts.html.

Chapter 2: Child Abuse

27. Quoted in U.S. Advisory Board on Child Abuse and Neglect, *A Nation's Shame: Fatal Child Abuse and Neglect in the United States.* Washington, DC: National Clearinghouse

on Child Abuse and Neglect, April 1995, p. 131.

28. Somers, *Wednesday's Children*, p. 28.

29. Quoted in Williams and Money, *Traumatic Abuse and Neglect of Children at Home*, p. 154.

30. Ray E. Helfer and Ruth S. Kempe, eds., *The Battered Child.* Chicago: University of Chicago Press, 1987, p. 73.

31. Quoted in Somers, *Wednesday's Children*, pp. 108–109.

32. Quoted in Somers, *Wednesday's Children*, p. 43.

33. Quoted in Williams and Money, *Traumatic Abuse and Neglect of Children at Home*, p. 25.

34. Quoted in Patricia A. Schene, "Past, Present, and Future Roles of Child Protective Services," *The Future of Children*, Spring 1998, p. 26.

35. Quoted in Jacquelyn McCroskey and William Meezan, "Family-Centered Services, Approaches, and Effectiveness," *The Future of Children*, Spring 1998, p. 59.

36. Quoted in Artenstein, *Runaways*, p. 3.

37. Quoted in Artenstein, *Runaways*, p. 34.

38. Charlene Ingram, "Kinship Care: From Last Resort to First Choice," *Child Welfare*, September/October 1996, p. 552.

39. U.S. Advisory Board on Child Abuse and Neglect, *A Nation's Shame*, p. 55.

Chapter 3: Domestic Violence

40. APA Presidential Task Force on Violence and the Family, *Violence and the Family*, p. 14.

41. Lundy Bancroft, *Why Does He Do That? Inside the Minds of Angry and Controlling Men.* New York: G.P. Putnam's Sons, 2002, p. 163.

42. APA Presidential Task Force on Violence and the Family, *Violence and the Family*, p. 112.

43. Bancroft, *Why Does He Do That?* p. 201.

44. Quoted in Statman, *The Battered Woman's Survival Guide*, p. 60.

45. Quoted in Statman, *The Battered Woman's Survival Guide*, p. 62.

46. Cantrell, *Into the Light*, p. 10.

47. Cantrell, *Into the Light*, p. 11.

48. Quoted in Deborah Sontag, "Bad Love," *New York Times Magazine*, November 17, 2002, p. 54.

49. Quoted in Somers, *Wednesday's Children*, p. 148.

50. Quoted in Statman, *The Battered Woman's Survival Guide*, p. 56.

51. Quoted in Ann Jones, *Next Time, She'll Be Dead: Battering and How to Stop It*. Boston: Beacon Press, 1994, p. 36.

52. Bancroft, *Why Does He Do That?* p. 352.

53. Statman, *The Battered Woman's Survival Guide*, p. 93.

54. Statman, *The Battered Woman's Survival Guide*, p. 88.

55. Kay Bartlett, "Spousal Homicide Law: 'Open Season' on Men or Domestic Violence?" *Los Angeles Times*, March 17, 1991, p. 33.

56. Quoted in Bartlett, "Spousal Homicide Law," p. 33.

57. Bancroft, *Why Does He Do That?* p. 294.

58. Quoted in Jones, *Next Time, She'll Be Dead*, p. 29.

59. Bancroft, *Why Does He Do That?* p. 335.

Chapter 4: Elder Abuse

60. Ola W. Barnett, Cindy L. Miller-Perrin, and Robin D. Perrin, *Family Violence Across the Lifespan: An Introduction*. Thousand Oaks, CA: Sage Publications, 1997, p. 255.

61. Barnett, Miller-Perrin, and Perrin, *Family Violence Across the Lifespan*, p. 255.

62. National Center on Elder Abuse, "The Basics: Major Types of Elder Abuse," p. 3. www.elderabusecenter.org/default.cfm?p=basics.cfm.

63. Holly Danks, "Risks of Elder Abuse Increasing," *Oregonian*, March 6, 2003, p. 1.

64. Rosalie S. Wolf and Karl A. Pillemer, *Helping Elderly*

Victims: The Reality of Elder Abuse. New York: Columbia University Press, 1989, p. 7.

65. Myrna Reis, "The IOA Screen: An Abuse-Alert Measure That Dispels Myths," *Generations*, Summer 2000, p. 16.

66. Quoted in American Medical Association, *Conference Proceedings: National Conference on Family Violence: Health and Justice.* Washington, DC: American Medical Association, March 11–13, 1994, p. 20.

67. Liz Taylor, "Vigilant, Caring Neighbors Can Save Elders from Abuse," *Seattle Times*, June 9, 2003, p. E5.

68. Quoted in Barnett, Miller-Perrin, and Perrin, *Family Violence Across the Lifespan*, p. 253.

69. Georgia J. Anetzberger, "Caregiving: Primary Cause of Elder Abuse?" *Generations*, Summer 2000, p. 49.

70. Mary Joy Quinn, "Undoing Undue Influence," *Generations*, Summer 2000, p. 65.

71. Quoted in Quinn, "Undoing Undue Influence," pp. 65–66.

72. Barnett, Miller-Perrin, and Perrin, *Family Violence Across the Lifespan*, p. 268.

73. Rosalie S. Wolf, "Introduction: The Nature and Scope of Elder Abuse," *Generations*, Summer 2000, p. 7.

Chapter 5: Protecting Families

74. Martha A. Matthews, "The Impact of Federal and State Laws on Children Exposed to Domestic Violence," *The Future of Children*, Winter 1999, p. 57.

75. Bancroft, *Why Does He Do That?* p. 268.

76. Quoted in Susan Murphy-Milano, *Defending Our Lives: Getting Away from Domestic Violence and Staying Safe.* New York: Doubleday Anchor Books, 1996, p. 147.

77. Quoted in Louis W. McHardy and Meredith Hofford, *Family Violence: Emerging Programs for Battered Mothers and Their Children.* Reno, NV: National Council of Juvenile and Family Court Judges, July 1998, p. 149.

78. Quoted in Statman, *The Battered Woman's Survival Guide*, p. 90.

79. Quoted in Mildred Daley Pagelow, "Commentary: Justice for Victims of Spouse Abuse in Divorce and Child Custody Cases," *Violence and Victims*, 1993, p. 74.

80. U.S. Advisory Board on Child Abuse and Neglect, *A Nation's Shame*, p. 50.

81. Quoted in McHardy and Hofford, *Family Violence*, p. 10.

82. Quoted in McHardy and Hofford, *Family Violence*, p. 10.

83. Quoted in McHardy and Hofford, *Family Violence*, p. 11.

84. McHardy and Hofford, *Family Violence*, pp. 17–18.

85. U.S. Advisory Board on Child Abuse and Neglect, *A Nation's Shame*, pp. 49–50.

86. Quoted in Somers, *Wednesday's Children*, p. 9.

87. Somers, *Wednesday's Children*, pp. 2–3.

Organizations to Contact

Administration on Aging

One Massachusetts Ave., Suites 4100 and 5100
Washington, DC 20201
(202) 619-0724
www.aoa.gov

A federal resource center for all types of aging issues, including elder abuse. Its mission is to bring together organizations and the public to meet the needs of older adults. The website has a wide variety of materials on elder abuse that are easy to read and informative.

Family Violence Prevention Fund

383 Rhode Island St., Suite 304
San Francisco, CA 94103
phone: (415) 252-8900
fax: (415) 252-8991
www.endabuse.org

The Family Violence Prevention Fund, a national nonprofit organization, focuses on preventing domestic violence through education and policy reform. It is a leader in the area of training medical providers to recognize and report family violence and in setting national policy. The website has a wide variety of materials and fact sheets.

Los Angeles Commision on Assaults Against Women (LACAAW)

605 W. Olympic Blvd., Suite 400
Los Angeles, CA 90015
phone: (213) 955-9090

fax: (213) 955-9093
24-hour hotlines: (310) 392-8381; (213) 626-3392;
(626) 793-3385
www.lacaaw.org

A nonprofit multicultural organization dedicated to eliminating violence against women, youth, and children. It runs a variety of programs designed to reduce domestic violence, including "In Touch with Teens." LACAAW has a department that focuses on teen relationship violence and runs a youth leadership program. The website has a youth-only section.

National Center on Elder Abuse

1201 15th St. NW, Suite 350
Washington, DC 20005
phone: (202) 898-2586
fax: (202) 898-2583
www.elderabusecenter.org

A national resource center that promotes understanding, knowledge, and action to prevent elder abuse, neglect, and exploitation. The center is funded by the National Association of State Units on Aging. It collaborates on research; provides consultation, education, and training; identifies and provides information about promising practices and interventions; answers inquiries and requests for information; and advises on program and policy development.

National Clearinghouse on Child Abuse and Neglect

330 C St. SW
Washington, DC 20447
toll free: (800) 394-3366
phone: (703) 385-7565
fax: (703) 385-3206
http://nccanch.acf.hhs.gov

A national clearinghouse for information on the prevention and treatment of child abuse and neglect, including statistics, a wide variety of publications, training materials, and lists of national and local organizations working to prevent child abuse and neglect. It also provides updates on current laws and promising practices.

National Council of Juvenile and Family Court Judges

Family Violence Department
PO Box 8970
Reno, NV 89507
toll free: (800) 527-3223
phone: (775) 784-6012
fax: (775) 784-6160
www.ncjfcj.org/dept/fvd

Operates a resource center and produces documents that discuss current issues and challenges to preventing family violence. Provides information, consultation, training, and legal research related to child protection and child custody.

National Resource Center on Domestic Violence

6400 Flank Dr., Suite 1300
Harrisburg, PA 17112
toll free: (800) 537-2238
www.nrcdv.org

This resource center, operated by the Pennsylvania Coalition Against Domestic Violence, provides a wide variety of information and resources on recent research, policy development, and training to enhance community response to domestic violence. It is designed as a national network to provide support to organizations and individuals to end violence in the lives of women and their children.

Texas Council on Family Violence

PO Box 161810
Austin, TX 78716
phone: (512) 794-1133
fax: (512) 794-1199
toll free: (800) 799-SAFE
www.tcfv.org

One of the largest domestic violence coalitions in the United States. It operates a multilingual twenty-four-hour hotline to provide crisis information and referrals to local programs. It assists battered women's shelters, advocates for policy, and has extensive resource files. The website contains a variety of information, and workers respond to requests for information.

For Further Reading

Maria Hong, *Family Abuse: A National Epidemic.* Springfield, NJ: Enslow, 1997. An overview of the problem of family violence, including child abuse; domestic violence; and elder, sibling, and parent abuse. Includes sections on society's role and where to find help.

Margaret O. Hyde, *Know About Abuse.* New York: Walker, 1992. An easy-to-read discussion of family violence, including physical, sexual, and emotional abuse. Examines how and why family violence occurs and suggests what you can do to help yourself or a friend.

Barrie Levy and Patricia Occhiuzzo Giggans, *What Parents Need to Know About Dating Violence.* Seattle: Seal Press, 1995. Written for parents, this book contains information on abusive relationships which is important for all teens to know. Easy to read with many true-life stories and lists to help identify abusive behavior in a relationship.

Susan Mufson and Rachel Kranz, *Straight Talk About Child Abuse.* New York: Facts On File, 1991. A straightforward presentation of the problem of child abuse, with a focus on the experience of teens. The extent of the problem, the impact of abuse, finding solutions, and where to get help are all discussed.

Susan Murphy-Milano, *Defending Our Lives: Getting Away from Domestic Violence and Staying Safe.* New York: Doubleday Anchor Books, 1996. Written by an abuse survivor who grew up witnessing domestic violence as a child and founded Project: Protect to help others survive. The author begins by sharing her own story. She then provides a comprehensive easy-to-read guide on how to protect yourself or help friends or family members survive domestic violence.

Works Consulted

Books

Jeffrey Artenstein, *Runaways: In Their Own Words: Kids Talking About Living on the Streets.* New York: Tom Doherty Associates, 1990. A collection of true-life stories describing the experiences of teenage runaways, many of whom have suffered abuse along the way. The book is easy to read, engaging, and thought provoking.

Lundy Bancroft, *Why Does He Do That? Inside the Minds of Angry and Controlling Men.* New York: G.P. Putnam's Sons, 2002. Written by an expert on domestic violence, this book provides insight into the thinking of abusive men and how that affects their partners. One of the clearest presentations of the power and control issues behind domestic violence. A bit more challenging to read, but worth it.

Ola W. Barnett, Cindy L. Miller-Perrin, and Robin D. Perrin, *Family Violence Across the Lifespan: An Introduction.* Thousand Oaks, CA: Sage Publications, 1997. An overview of the field of family violence with interviews of key researchers in the field. This book is both academic and technical.

Leslie A. Cantrell, *Into the Light: A Guide for Battered Women.* Edmonds, WA: Charles Franklin Press, 1986. A short, twenty-eight-page book that is designed to help battered women understand domestic violence and take steps to ensure their safety and recovery from abuse. It has some technical language but contains a clear presentation of the problem of domestic violence and what actions a battered woman can take to protect herself and her children.

Patricia Evans, *The Verbally Abusive Relationship: How to Recognize It and How to Respond.* Holbrook, MA: Bob

Adams, 1992. A description of verbal abuse, including checklists to help the reader determine if he or she is being verbally abused. Later chapters discuss power and control and how to respond to verbal abuse.

Ray E. Helfer and Ruth S. Kempe, eds., *The Battered Child.* Chicago: University of Chicago Press, 1987. This classic text on child abuse is a collection of articles by child abuse experts. Highly technical, for academicians.

Ann Jones, *Next Time, She'll Be Dead: Battering and How to Stop It.* Boston: Beacon Press, 1994. A review of the police, court, and media response to battered women and their attempts to live free of abuse. A damning picture of society's response to victims and survivors of domestic violence. Written for the lay public.

Barrie Levy, ed., *Dating Violence: Young Women in Danger.* Seattle: Seal Press, 1991. Presents personal stories of teens involved in violent relationships, an academic look at the problems teens face, and a discussion of community and school-based programs to address the problem of violence in teen relationships.

Ginger Rhodes and Richard Rhodes, *Trying to Get Some Dignity: Stories of Triumph over Childhood Abuse.* New York: William Morrow, 1996. True-life stories from survivors of child abuse. Told in vignettes and interviews with the authors.

Patricia R. Salber and Ellen Taliaferro, *The Physician's Guide to Domestic Violence: How to Ask the Right Questions and Recognize Abuse.* Volcano, CA: Volcano Press, 1995. A short, concise, easy-to-read discussion of domestic violence with specific information designed to help doctors ask questions of their patients in order to identify and help patients who are being abused.

Suzanne Somers, *Wednesday's Children: Adult Survivors of Abuse Speak Out.* New York: Jove/Healing Vision, 1993. A collection of true-life stories of famous people, mostly from the entertainment industry, who were abused as children. Easy to read, but the stories can be emotionally painful.

Jan Berliner Statman, *The Battered Woman's Survival Guide: Breaking the Cycle.* Dallas: Taylor, 1990. A clear overview of domestic violence designed for battered women, their families, and friends. Easy to read; contains both general information about domestic violence and specific information to help a battered woman determine if she is being abused, what she can do, and where to go for help.

Gertrude J. Williams and John Money, eds., *Traumatic Abuse and Neglect of Children at Home.* Baltimore, MD: Johns Hopkins University Press, 1980. A collection of articles written by child abuse experts and researchers. Highly technical, for academicians.

Rosalie S. Wolf and Karl A. Pillemer, *Helping Elderly Victims: The Reality of Elder Abuse.* New York: Columbia University Press, 1989. Reviews the history and problem of elder abuse, with a focus on specific research conducted by the authors. Academic, with some technical chapters.

Periodicals

Georgia J. Anetzberger, "Caregiving: Primary Cause of Elder Abuse?" *Generations*, Summer 2000.

Kay Bartlett, "Spousal Homicide Law: 'Open Season' on Men or Domestic Violence?" *Los Angeles Times*, March 17, 1991.

Suzanne Beck, "Dixon Resident Embezzles $41,000," *California Aggie*, August 11, 2003.

L. Rene Bergeron and Betsey Gray, "Ethical Dilemmas of Reporting Suspected Elder Abuse," *Social Work*, January 2003.

Jill Duerr Berrick, "When Children Cannot Remain Home: Foster Family Care and Kinship Care," *The Future of Children*, Spring 1998.

Bonnie Brandl, "Power and Control: Understanding Domestic Abuse in Later Life," *Generations*, Summer 2000.

Holly Danks, "Risks of Elder Abuse Increasing," *Oregonian*, March 6, 2003.

Carmel Bitondo Dyer and Angela M. Goins, "The Role of the Interdisciplinary Geriatric Assessment in Addressing Self-Neglect of the Elderly," *Generations*, Summer 2000.

Diana J. English, "The Extent and Consequences of Child Maltreatment," *The Future of Children*, Spring 1998.

Candace J. Heisler, "Elder Abuse and the Criminal Justice System: New Awareness, New Responses," *Generations*, Summer 2000.

Merry Hofford et al., "Family Violence in Child Custody Statutes: An Analysis of State Codes and Legal Practice," *Family Law Quarterly*, Summer 1995.

Charlene Ingram, "Kinship Care: From Last Resort to First Choice," *Child Welfare*, September/October 1996.

Tanya Fusco Johnson, "Ethics in Addressing Mistreatment of Elders: Can We Have Ethics for All?" *Generations*, Summer 2000.

Jane F. Knapp, "The Impact of Children Witnessing Violence," *Pediatric Clinics of North America*, April 1998.

Martha A. Matthews, "The Impact of Federal and State Laws on Children Exposed to Domestic Violence," *The Future of Children*, Winter 1999.

Jacquelyn McCroskey and William Meezan, "Family-Centered Services, Approaches, and Effectiveness," *The Future of Children*, Spring 1998.

Ailee Moon, "Perceptions of Elder Abuse Among Various Cultural Groups: Similarities and Differences," *Generations*, Summer 2000.

National Center on Elder Abuse, *Reporting of Elder Abuse in Domestic Settings*, Elder Abuse Information Series no. 3, November 1997.

———, *Trends in Elder Abuse in Domestic Settings*, Elder Abuse Information Series no. 2, November 1997.

———, *Types of Elder Abuse in Domestic Settings*, Elder

Abuse Information Series no. 1, March 1999.

Daniel Nelson, "Violence Against Elderly People: A Neglected Problem," *Lancet*, October 5, 2002.

Lisa Nerenberg, "Developing a Service Response to Elder Abuse," *Generations*, Summer 2000.

Joanne Marlatt Otto, "The Role of Adult Protective Services in Addressing Abuse," *Generations*, Summer 2000.

Mildred Daley Pagelow, "Commentary: Justice for Victims of Spouse Abuse in Divorce and Child Custody Cases," *Violence and Victims*, 1993.

Mary Joy Quinn, "Undoing Undue Influence," *Generations*, Summer 2000.

Holly Ramsey-Klawsnik, "Elder-Abuse Offenders: A Typology," *Generations*, Summer 2000.

Myrna Reis, "The IOA Screen: An Abuse-Alert Measure That Dispels Myths," *Generations*, Summer 2000.

Amy J. Saathoff and Elizabeth Ann Stoffel, "Community-Based Domestic Violence Services," *The Future of Children*, Winter 1999.

Daniel G. Saunders, "Child Custody Decisions in Families Experiencing Woman Abuse," *Social Work*, January 1994.

Patricia A. Schene, "Past, Present, and Future Roles of Child Protective Services," *The Future of Children*, Spring 1998.

Deborah Sontag, "Bad Love," *New York Times Magazine*, November 17, 2002.

Lori Stiegel, "The Changing Role of the Courts in Elder-Abuse Cases," *Generations*, Summer 2000.

Liz Taylor, "Vigilant, Caring Neighbors Can Save Elders from Abuse," *Seattle Times*, June 9, 2003.

Rosalie S. Wolf, "Introduction: The Nature and Scope of Elder Abuse," *Generations*, Summer 2000.

Internet Sources

American College of Obstetricians and Gynecologists, "Fact Sheet: Interpersonal Violence Against Women Throughout the Life Span." www.acog.org/from_home/departments/category.cfm?recno-17&bulletin-186.

American Psychological Association, "Facts About Family Violence," 2003. www.apa.org/releases/facts.html.

Bonnie Brandl and Loree Cook-Daniels, "Domestic Abuse in Later Life," *National Electronic Network on Violence Against Women*, December 2002. www.vawnet.org/DomesticViolence/Research/VAWnetDocs/AR_later-life.php.

Centers for Disease Control and Prevention, National Center for Injury Prevention and Control, "The Co-Occurrence of Intimate Partner Violence Against Mothers and Abuse of Children." www.cdc.gov/ncipc/factsheets/dvcan.htm.

———, "Intimate Partner Violence." www.cdc.gov/ncipc/factsheets/ipvfacts.htm.

———, "Male Batterers." www.cdc.gov/ncipc/factsheets/malebat.htm.

Family Violence Prevention Fund, "Domestic Violence Is a Serious, Widespread Social Problem in America: The Facts." http://endabuse.org/programs/printable/display.php3?DocID=174.

———, "Get the Facts—Domestic Violence and Children." http://endabuse.org/programs/printable/display.php3?DocID=77.

———, "Get the Facts—Domestic Violence and Health Care." http://endabuse.org/programs/printable/display.php3?DocID=25.

Mary E. Gilfus, "Women's Experiences of Abuse as a Risk Factor for Incarceration," *National Electronic Network on Violence Against Women*, December 2002. www.vawnet.org/DomesticViolence/Research/VAWnetDocs/AR_Incarceration.php.

Liz Claiborne Inc. and the Family Violence Prevention Fund, *A Woman's Handbook: A Practical Guide to Discussing Relationship Abuse and What You Need to Know About Dating Violence.* www.lizclaiborne.com/lizinc/lizworks/women/person.asp.

Liz Claiborne Women's Work, *A Parent's Guide to Teen Dating Violence: 10 Questions to Start the Conversation,* New York: Liz Claiborne, Inc., 2001. www.lizclaiborne.com/lizinc/lizworks/women/pdf/10questions_hand.pdf.

————, *What You Need to Know About Dating Violence: A Teen's Handbook*, New York: Liz Claiborne, Inc., 2001. www.lizclaiborne.com/lizinc/lizworks/women/pdf/teen_hand book.pdf.

National Center on Elder Abuse, "The Basics: Major Types of Elder Abuse." www.elderabusecenter.org/default.cfm?p=basics.cfm.

————, "Elder Abuse Awareness Kit," 2003. www.elderabuse center.org.

————, "Risk Factors for Elder Abuse." www.elderabuse center.org/default.cfm?p=riskfactors.cfm.

National Clearinghouse on Child Abuse and Neglect Information, "In Harm's Way: Domestic Violence and Child Maltreatment." October 1998. http://nccanch.acf.hhs.gov/pubs/otherpubs/ harmsway.cfm.

————, "Child Maltreatment 2001: Summary of Key Findings," October 2003. http://nccanch.acf.hhs.gov/pubs/factsheets/ canstats.cfm.

————, "Prevention Pays: The Costs of Not Preventing Child Abuse and Neglect," February 2003. http://nccanch.acf.hhs.gov/pubs/prevenres/pays.cfm.

Daniel G. Saunders, "Child Custody and Visitation Decisions in Domestic Violence Cases: Legal Trends, Research Findings, and Recommendations," *National Electronic Network on Violence Against Women*, August

1998. www.vawnet.org/DomesticViolence/Research/VAWnet Docs/AR_custody.php.

U.S. Department of Health and Human Services, Administration on Aging, "Fact Sheets: Elder Abuse Prevention." www.aoa.gov/press/fact/alpha/fact_elder_abuse.asp.

Government and Professional Association Documents

American Medical Association, *Conference Proceedings: National Conference on Family Violence: Health and Justice*. Washington, DC: American Medical Association, March 11–13, 1994.

American Psychological Association Presidential Task Force on Violence and the Family, *Violence and the Family.* Washington, DC: American Psychological Association, 1996.

Richard J. Bonnie and Robert B. Wallace, eds., *Elder Mistreatment: Abuse, Neglect, and Exploitation in an Aging America.* Washington, DC: National Academies Press, 2003.

Kathleen Chamberlin, Sheila Anderson, and Dawn Marie Wadle, *Home Visitor's Guidebook: Domestic and Other Family Violence.* Sacramento, CA: Community College Foundation, 2001.

Barbara Cottrell, *Parent Abuse: The Abuse of Parents by Their Teenage Children.* Ottawa, Canada: National Clearinghouse on Family Violence, Family Violence Prevention Unit, Health Canada, 2001.

Barbara Hart, "Battered Women and the Duty to Protect Children." In *State Codes on Domestic Violence: Analysis, Commentary, and Recommendations.* Reno, NV: National Council of Juvenile and Family Court Judges, 1990.

Louis W. McHardy and Meredith Hofford, *Family Violence: Emerging Programs for Battered Mothers and Their Children.* Reno, NV: National Council of Juvenile and Family Court Judges, July 1998.

Susan Schechter and Jeffrey L. Edleson, *Effective Intervention in Domestic Violence and Child Maltreatment Cases: Guidelines for Policy and Practice.* Reno, NV: National Council of Juvenile and Family Court Judges, 1999.

Pamela B. Teaster, *A Response to the Abuse of Vulnerable Adults: The 2000 Survey of State Adult Protective Services.* Washington, DC: National Center on Elder Abuse, November 2002.

Patricia Tjaden and Nancy Thoennes, *Extent, Nature, and Consequences of Intimate Partner Violence: Findings from the National Violence Against Women Survey.* Washington, DC: U.S. Department of Justice, National Institute of Justice, Office of Justice Programs, July 2000.

Leslie Tutty, *Husband Abuse: An Overview of Research and Perspectives.* Ottawa, Canada: Family Violence Prevention Unit, Health Canada, 1999.

U.S. Advisory Board on Child Abuse and Neglect, *A Nation's Shame: Fatal Child Abuse and Neglect in the United States.* Washington, DC: National Clearinghouse on Child Abuse and Neglect, April 1995.

U.S. Department of Health and Human Services, Administration on Children, Youth, and Families, *Child Maltreatment 2000.* Washington, DC: U.S. Government Printing Office, 2002.

Index

Picture Credits

About the Author

Janice M. Yuwiler, MPH, is the former director of the California Center for Childhood Injury Prevention. She consults for the Center for Injury Prevention Policy and Practice of the Graduate School of Public Health at San Diego State University. Yuwiler is a native Californian who enjoys living in beautiful Southern California with her husband and three children.